Praise for *Dare*

“Melissa has a wonderful way of maki
alive, not only in our heads but also in our hearts.”

—Marilyn Hontz
author of *Shame Lifter* and *Listening for God*

“The message of HOPE right now is countercultural, and God’s people can be viral kingdom agents with this message. Melissa Spoelstra helps us understand how critical Jeremiah’s words are for us. Her deeply personal and insightful treatment of these scriptures makes them more relevant than today’s news.”

—Reggie McNeal
author of *Kingdom Conspirators* and *Kingdom Come*

DARE TO *Hope*

LIVING INTENTIONALLY in an Unstable World

MELISSA SPOELSTRA

Abingdon Press
Nashville

DARE TO HOPE
LIVING INTENTIONALLY IN AN UNSTABLE WORLD

Library of Congress Cataloging-in-Publication Data has been requested.

ISBN 978-1-5018-7965-4

19 20 21 22 23 24 25 26 27 28—10 9 8 7 6 5 4 3 2 1

MANUFACTURED IN THE UNITED STATES OF AMERICA

For Sean.

Daring to hope alongside you has been a roller coaster, but my grandma was right. When she first met you, she said life with you would never be boring; and it has proved true. Thanks for loving me so well and showing me Jesus with skin on time after time. You are forever hopeful, and I love that about you!

Contents

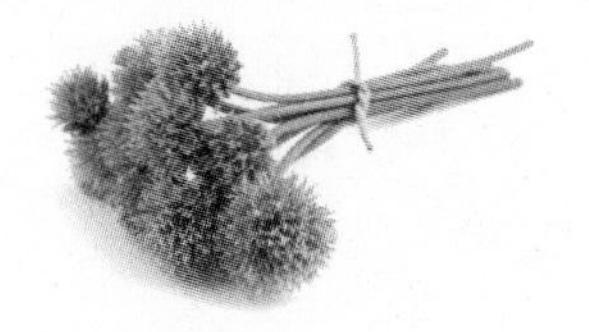

Introduction

When we look around at today's world, hope usually isn't the first word that comes to mind. In many ways we live in an age of uncertainty. If we allow our thoughts to linger on things such as the national debt, the condition of the environment, the increase in violence toward even our most innocent, and the looming moral bankruptcy of our culture, we can get pretty discouraged. The situation only compounds when we add our personal issues to these corporate ones. Life can be rough. When marriages fail, bank accounts run low, friendships end, or the everyday demands of a fast-paced life get us down, we sometimes feel the ground shaking beneath our feet.

Living in such an unstable world can give us a propensity to worry. Other choices of fear, doubt, and bitterness call us to select their posture when life gets overwhelming. Yet God offers us another choice. Through Him we can dare to hope—not in the government, our family, a job, or even the church. God calls us to surrender our wills to His and rest our hope in Him alone.

Sometimes I get moving through life at a breakneck pace and forget to be daring with hope. I command the calendar, devote time to work and ministry, juggle the kids' schedules, do some laundry, take care of other chores and errands, make plans for dinner, check in with friends, and then get up tomorrow and start all over again. I need a caution light as I'm racing through life to wake me up and say, "Slow down and pay attention!"

I got one of these wake-up calls one day while driving. Instead of a caution light, I got a caution bump. I had just dropped my girls off at a school activity and was on my way home. Earlier I had dumped out my purse on the passenger seat, frantically looking for something I needed at a moment's notice.

Now I was stopped at a red light, and I leaned over to put things back in my purse. Suddenly I felt a huge jolt as my van bumped into the minivan in front of me. I slammed the brake down hard, backed up, and went to talk to the woman in front of me. Thankfully, there was no damage to either car, but as I finished the short drive home, I was a little shaken. How could my foot have let up on the brake without me even realizing it? I was so caught up in my task that I slowly let the car slide forward without even being aware of what I was doing.

I laughed with God as I thought about what He was showing me: I need to pay attention to really important things instead of letting a small distraction put me in danger of hurting myself and others. This is so true in my spiritual life too. The minutia of day-to-day life as well as the trials that so frequently present themselves put me in danger of missing the hope in God's plans for me.

A similar wake-up call came in my life several years ago as I studied the Book of Jeremiah and discovered the words of the prophet echoing into my life and our culture with great relevance. This prophet found himself in a nation known for materialism, economic crisis, political globalization, and religious plurality. Sound familiar?

Much of the content in this book is drawn from the lessons God taught me then as I wrote the Bible study *Jeremiah: Daring to Hope in an Unstable World*, which continues to be going strong because hope is something we still desperately need in our world today. And there are no signs that is going to change! My prayer is that by sharing these insights in this new format, God's message of hope will reach even more people. Each chapter ends with a Dare to Hope challenge, and there are Scripture memory verses and practical helps at the end of the book.

A number of years ago, Francis Schaeffer said it this way,

> What, then should be our message in such a world—to the world, to the church, and to ourselves?
>
> We do not have to guess what God would say about this because there was a period of history, biblical history, which greatly parallels our day. That is the day of Jeremiah. The book of Jeremiah and the book of Lamentations show how God looks at a culture which knew Him and deliberately turned away.[1]

In the Book of Jeremiah, God calls out to His people, continually asking them to place their hope in Him instead of political alliances, material possessions, and people. Jeremiah gets his reputation as the "weeping prophet" honestly as he delivers weighty messages full of bad news and cautions for living. Yet if we are willing to look beneath the surface of God's warnings to His heart of love behind them, we find this underlying message:

Hope-filled living is possible even in an unstable world!

But how do we do this? Where do we start? That is what we will be considering together in this book. In the following chapters, we'll explore six incredibly relevant themes that lift right off the pages of Jeremiah's manuscript, providing six practical guidelines for hope-filled living:

1. Surrender
2. Reject Counterfeits
3. Listen
4. Check Your Heart
5. Take Personal Responsibility
6. Pursue Intimacy with God

We'll discover that Jeremiah's message was not a popular one. Unfortunately, the people of Judah did not see the hope in God's plans for them, and they did not heed Jeremiah's warnings. Their failure to make life changes in light of God's call to hope in Him led to exile. My prayer is that we will not be like them. I pray that God's timeless truths from this ancient book will help us take a careful look at our lives as we slow down and examine where we might be off course and how we can get back on track.

God is calling us to open our ears to Him. He knows life can throw us curveballs, and He knows how easy it is to get swept away with the cultural current of despair. Jeremiah dared to hope—even when his family rejected him. He lost his home and was mocked, imprisoned, and unjustly accused. He lost friends and finances. His circumstances remained bitter, but he learned to keep his heart soft and hopeful in the midst of tough stuff. That is my prayer for you and for me, that we can dare to hope no matter what we face. I pray that we may we be able to say with Jeremiah:

Yet I still dare to hope
when I remember this:

The faithful love of the LORD never ends!
His mercies never cease.
Great is his faithfulness;
his mercies begin afresh each morning.
(Lamentations 3:21-23)

If you are in need of fresh mercies today as I am, then I dare you to hope!

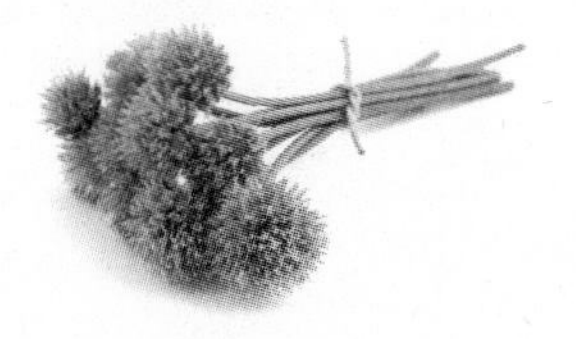

CHAPTER 1

Raising the White Flag

Surrender

When I discovered your words, I devoured them.
They are my joy and my heart's delight,
for I bear your name,
O Lord God of Heaven's Armies.
—Jeremiah 15:16

My husband and I discovered in our first year of marriage that doing home projects together is dangerous. When we tried to put up a wallpaper border in a bedroom, we had some pretty rough interactions. The root issue stems from both of us being control freaks. We like to lead and direct how things go. This can be a good thing in certain situations like when God has called us to lead, but when we have different ideas about anything from parenting to finances, our controlling natures war against each other. After several decades of marriage, I hope we have made some progress in the area of compromise—at least in the domain of painting walls and organizing the garage.

Being a control freak can get me in trouble in the spiritual realm as well. When life seems to be going as I think it should and God's instructions through His Spirit and His Word make sense to me, then I don't have to be daring with hope. However, I find more often that life feels complicated and often God's instructions take faith rather than sight to obey. It is during these seasons that I must raise the white flag and surrender to God's way.

The prophet Jeremiah experienced some instructions from God that didn't follow the rules of logic. God told him to hide underwear, speak bold messages, and identify counterfeits in the lives of the political and spiritual leaders of his day. I can't imagine what this would have been like when he was first called to deliver God's message of surrender as a boy of likely fourteen or fifteen years old. Though we might think that Jeremiah and other prophets of the Bible were super righteous, had it all together, and never struggled, the truth is that they were normal people like you and me. Jeremiah got depressed, made excuses, and even did some whining occasionally. But there is something that sets him apart from most of us: his unrelenting commitment to communicate God's message. You might say that Jeremiah was both deep and relatable!

Although Jeremiah's words resound from over twenty-six hundred years ago, they echo into our day with uncanny relevance. Our world is rife with greed, poverty, injustice, racism, and oppression, just to name a few of the challenges and battles. So what is our message to the world, and how do we go about sharing that message? To answer that question, we can look to the prophets—whose message, the disciple Peter said, is the light our dark world needs:

> Because of that great experience, we have even greater confidence in the message proclaimed by the prophets. You must pay close attention to what they wrote, for their words are like a lamp shining in a dark place—until the Day dawns, and Christ the Morning Star shines in your hearts. Above all, you must realize that no prophecy in Scripture ever came from the prophet's own understanding, or from human initiative. No, those prophets were

> moved by the Holy Spirit, and they spoke from God. (2 Peter 1:19-21)

When we pay close attention to the writings of the prophet Jeremiah, we discover that the changing of a culture starts with those who are living within it. If we long to see a turning back to God in our land, then we need to recognize that it starts with us—with you and with me. Not only does Jeremiah's prophecy matter today; God Himself gives us some direct instructions regarding how we should respond to it. Let's unpack a few of these together.

Surrendering Our Excuses

Jeremiah is the longest and what most consider to be one of the most disorganized books—chronologically speaking—in Scripture. We might find ourselves throwing in the towel and assuming that we don't have the biblical expertise to read Jeremiah, thinking, *It's too hard to understand; I don't know the geography or cultural context; how am I supposed to relate it to my life?* But as Peter's words remind us, we must pay close attention to what the prophets have to say to us—even now. And when we do, we will find direction regarding God's call on our lives.

We are not alone in our timidity to dig in to God's messages about our call. As a matter of fact, the Book of Jeremiah begins with a glimpse into his own tendency to excuse his ability to obey God's call. Jeremiah was the son of a priest living in the small town of Anathoth in the land of Benjamin, the least significant of the twelve tribes of Israel. We might compare it to the suburb of a bustling city with the lowest real estate values. It wouldn't have been the hot spot with the incredible school districts and rule-filled HOAs!

Jeremiah emerged during a time of great political upheaval. Babylon, Egypt, and Assyria rivaled for world domination, and the land of Judah was shuffled back and forth between them as vassals paying tribute to keep from being destroyed. It was in this climate, during the thirteenth year of King Josiah's reign in the land of Judah, that God called Jeremiah to deliver His messages.

In the very first chapter God speaks kindly to Jeremiah, saying that God knew him and set him apart for this work before he was even born (v. 5). Psalm 139 gives a similar picture from David's pen:

> You made all the delicate, inner parts of my body
> and knit me together in my mother's womb.
> Thank you for making me so wonderfully complex!
> Your workmanship is marvelous—how well I
> know it. (vv. 13-14)

Now, Jeremiah did not hear God's precious words and say, "Yes, sign me up!" He had some reservations about speaking God's messages to the people of Judah, just as we might. He was too young and couldn't speak well. And remember the small town and the least tribe that he came from? Who was he to speak for God to a culture that wasn't listening? He was more than just concerned about his ability to be used by God, set apart from the womb or not.

We, too, make our fair share of excuses when it comes to obeying God. I know I have come up with some good ones: I'm both too old and too young, I don't have time, and I am not qualified. At times I've felt nudges to do something outside of my comfort zone for God only to talk myself out of it. As a young mom, I started writing some articles but convinced myself no one would want to read what I had written. In Christian circles, ambition to do something big can be labeled as pride or self-promotion. Somehow we convince ourselves that humility means staying under the radar and not attempting anything great for God. Like Jeremiah, we want an "out" to disobey. Perhaps you're nodding your head in agreement right now. Or you might be thinking, *I'm not sure God has ever called me to do anything!* But the reality is that God has a calling on each of our lives. Let's look at what He asked of Jeremiah to see if it might speak to our own call from God.

In the simplest of terms, God asked Jeremiah to speak His messages; and, in fact, God's mission for us as followers of Jesus is very similar to that call. God wants us to go when and where He sends, speak His words, and prepare for action without fear. But let's be honest. How many people do you know who actually live like this, ready to follow God whenever to wherever, no matter the task? If you're like me, you might be prone to give up with the least amount of resistance. Insecurity and fear of failure can keep us from trying new things. We wonder if others will think we are prideful. We question if we really heard God correctly. But the good news is that God knows following Him can be scary for us in our humanness. That's why He told Jeremiah twice in chapter 1, "Do not be afraid" (vv. 8, 17). And like Jeremiah, God wants us to face our fears and trust Him.

Many Christians today often have a difficult time saying yes to big things for God—and women in particular can struggle with this. Dr. Jennifer Degler, coauthor of the book *No More Christian Nice Girl*, says, "Many times we find that women get a pass on not being courageous.... We want to call that 'having a gentle and kind spirit,' but really it can be timidity or fear that's holding us back."[1] We also can neglect to encourage others to step out in faith with bold moves. The success of another—or even the potential that another might be greatly used of God—can threaten our own sense of worth, so we sometimes talk each other down. Instead we should be encouraging each other to listen to God and then step out in obedience. I know I need that; don't you?

Thankfully, God understands that His callings can be scary. He doesn't give us marching orders and a slap on the back and then fling us out to figure things out on our own. As we see in His words to Jeremiah in chapter 1, God tells us to be brave, assuring us that He will be with us and fight for us (vv. 17-19). He will take care of us even when the task seems too big for us, always assuring us that He will not leave us without His help.

Let this sink in: *God has a purpose for each of our lives.* He not only has a purpose for us; He has *big plans* for us! Sadly, we often miss it because of our own fear, insecurity, and excuses. As Craig Groeschel says in *The Christian Atheist*, "Before you can tap into God's life-changing power, you have to eliminate the excuses."[2] Excuses keep us from daring to do what God has called us to do. But when we raise the white flag of surrender—letting go of all our excuses, saying yes to God, and trusting Him—we get to experience the power of God at work in our lives. Incredible!

Surrendering Recognition and Popularity

In addition to the instruction to surrender our excuses, we find in Jeremiah's writings wisdom regarding the need to surrender our desire for recognition and acceptance. This is a message that goes against the grain of our culture.

When I was in junior high, my mom told me not to worry about popularity because once you leave high school, no one cares about that stuff anymore. She was wrong! I see it in the neighborhood. I see

When we raise the white flag
of surrender
—letting go of all our excuses,
saying yes to God, and trusting Him—
we get to experience the power of God
at work in our lives.

it at PTO meetings. I see it in the church. We size each other up all the time. A blend of confidence, money, career success, appearance, education, and experience (even in ministry) all contribute to our "status" in whatever social circles we run. If anything, it gets more complicated as we grow older. We are still trying to find the right "lunch table" at every stage of life. Can you relate?

We learn from Jeremiah that God is not as concerned about our popularity as He is with our faithfulness to His message. While earlier God had told the people of Israel through Joshua to go in and take the Promised Land, we see that God gave a very different message through the prophet Jeremiah: admit defeat without a fight. Though the messages were different, the importance of responding faithfully was the same.

In Jeremiah's case, his words failed to win him popularity with the people, and we can understand why. Imagine the day the twin towers of the World Trade Center fell. Now pretend the people responsible for such brutality launched a full-scale attack upon our land. Suppose one of the great Christian leaders of our day began preaching that we should admit defeat without a fight. To say that we would resist that message is an understatement, right?

Remember that Jeremiah was the young, unknown son of a priest from a small town and tribe. No wonder he didn't jump up and down at the task set before him. His message foretold the destruction of their communities. Yet despite the risk and cost, Jeremiah faithfully proclaimed God's words over and over, and he began to get a reputation as a prophet of doom and gloom. This didn't go over well with the government officials.

Babylon was nipping at Judah's heels, demanding tribute, taking their best people (like Daniel), and threatening total destruction.

Jeremiah's suggestion to fully give in didn't sit well with a government that was trying to rally its fighting men and boost morale.

In our lives as well, the message of surrender is not as popular as the message of victory. We want God to fix our circumstances and tell us everything is going to work out fine. We want our money problems solved, our physical illnesses healed, and our relationships simplified. Though sometimes God chooses to intervene in those ways, other times He calls us to surrender—such as allowing us to endure health challenges, grow through relational conflict, and learn to look for eternal blessings while temporal ones persist. But ultimately, God gives us victory through that surrender. He teaches us things, develops our character, and draws us close to Him through our struggles.

These prophecies in Jeremiah give us more than just a history of how Judah rebelled against God and faced punishment. While their story warns us to live righteous lives in obedience to God, it teaches us so much more, pointing us toward surrender to God's plan and purpose in the overarching biblical story. In fact, the last pages of the canonical Word drive home this truth: *God's intent in prophecy is to give us a clear picture of our Messiah.* Jesus is all over the pages of Jeremiah from start to finish! Although it may come in whispers, hints, foreshadowing, and messianic prophecies, we now have the fullness of God's Word and the hindsight to connect the spiritual dots; and we can praise God for allowing us to live at a time in history with access to so much of His truth at our fingertips.

The New Testament sheds further light on how the gospel carries a message of surrender. Jesus calls us, His followers, to deny ourselves and take up our crosses (Luke 9:23), essentially calling us to surrender. This message of surrender is not a "one-time" salvation experience. Rather, it is a daily call to surrender—and it can look different for different people. This is so important for us to take to heart and remember daily.

I recall a time when I was asking God to lead me in whether to help a single mom on welfare by taking her to lunch and giving her a gift card. My close friend who had a connection with her before I did felt that we should demonstrate tough love and not enable her because of some particular choices she had made recently. I struggled. I prayed. I read Scripture to look for guidance. I asked God to confirm His leading. As a consummate people-pleaser, it was hard for me to surrender to God's call to help the woman when I knew my friend might not be happy with my decision. She truly wanted to help the woman as well but felt that God was calling her to keep her distance. In this instance, the call to surrender looked different for each of us. (Incidentally, my friend ended up being totally fine with my decision; the battle was more in my insecurity than in reality.)

Just as God called John the Baptist to fast and Jesus to feast, He sometimes has us follow different directions for His purposes. The key is to stay close to Him so that we can hear. While God led His people to go in and conquer the land with Joshua, through Jeremiah His message was "surrender."

Maybe even now you are sensing God's call to surrender—perhaps by making amends with someone you are at odds with, by taking the leap to begin tithing to your church, by getting up earlier so you can pray, by obeying Christ in an area that you know won't be popular, or by becoming involved in or stepping down from a ministry because God says to. Whatever the specific call, we can know and rely on the fact that God will be with us in every faith-filled, obedient step.

Surrendering When Life Happens

So, we hear God's call or voice and we surrender. Sounds simple, right? Actually, acting on God's call and obeying God's message of surrender take faith and obedience. And once we've taken that step of surrender, it is often tested by fire. Sometimes even when we obey completely, we still end up in a pit. When my husband and I sensed the Lord calling him to plant a new church, we found confirmation as people joined our team and someone gave a large financial gift to get us started. It felt like such an adventure in the early days with all the new possibilities on the horizon. While we've seen God do amazing things in the season of church planting, we also spent many days in what seemed like a pit. Strained friendships, complaints, and misunderstandings made us want to give up and surrender to despair rather than to Jesus at times.

The pit, or cistern, was literal for Jeremiah. As we read in Jeremiah 38:4-6, the king's officials actually threw Jeremiah in a pit of mud. Now, a cistern was essentially a large pit that was cut into a rock and covered with a plaster made of mud. The people used cisterns to collect rainwater in the winter that they could use in the arid months of summer. We read that this particular cistern was actually so deep that Jeremiah had to be lowered into it by ropes. (Imagine the sinking feeling he must have had—literally!) We also discover that there was no water in this cistern—probably due to little rainfall—though there was some mud at the bottom from whatever rain there had been. Jeremiah could starve or freeze waiting for death in this solitary place.

Though we've probably never found ourselves in a literal pit facing death, we can relate to being in a pit of despair and hopelessness because of our circumstances. Often when we commit to obey or deliver God's message, life still happens. Friends betray us. Husbands leave. Children go astray. Jobs are lost. Health declines instead of improves. These are the times when we must trust God's greater plan even though our circumstances are screaming foul.

You might be thinking, *But obedience should be rewarded, right?* Jeremiah honestly dialogued with God over questions such as this; yet, ultimately, he surrendered to God's way even when it made no human sense. And as we continue reading his story, we see that it didn't end in the bottom of a cistern. He had a friend in the king's court who pleaded for him, and eventually he gained the ear of the king himself. Talk about hope!

When we are in the pit despite our obedience, we must continue to surrender to God. And when we are experiencing difficulty *because* of our obedience, as Jeremiah was, God says we actually have cause to be happy—for Jesus says when this happens, your reward in heaven will be great (Matthew 5:11-12). In those times we can remember Jeremiah's unpopular message and rough times and then recall God's faithfulness to take care of him, trusting God to do the same for us.

Jeremiah told the people that God wanted to save and rescue them, but first they had to surrender. Similarly, we need to yield completely to Christ. He wants to give us rich, satisfying, abundant life (John 10:10), and He knows we won't find it apart from Him. As Jeremiah discovered, surrendering to God brings peace and purpose even in the midst of terrifying circumstances. Sometimes all we need is a little reassurance.

Asking for Confirmation

Jeremiah was chosen as God's anointed prophet and spent a lifetime writing the words now contained in the book identified by his name—a total of around ninety separate revelations from God over a span of forty years. As I read Jeremiah's writings, I am amazed how boldly he proclaimed God's messages. Over and over he said things such as "Then the Lord spoke to me again," "The Lord gave me another message," "Then the Lord said to me," "This is what the Lord says." How could Jeremiah share God's words so confidently? Did God speak to him with an audible voice? Were the words written out for him like the Ten Commandments carved in stone? Or was it an unmistakable inner voice saying, "Jeremiah, I have another message for you"? What enabled him to trust that he had heard God clearly and correctly? Didn't he ever doubt?

Since Jeremiah was just as human as we are, I would imagine that he doubted and needed reassurance just as we do. The secret of Jeremiah's confidence and the reason he was able to speak with assurance is that he allowed God to confirm His messages. Let's glimpse into Jeremiah's intimate prayer life and look for specific ways he knew God was speaking to him.

We see in Jeremiah 20 that the priest in charge of the Temple, Pashhur, had just learned of Jeremiah's prophecy calling for surrender and defeat. He arrested Jeremiah and had him whipped and put in stocks—not the outcome Jeremiah had hoped for, I'm sure! Although Jeremiah was released the next day and continued to preach destruction, he had some heavy questions for his Lord; and he talked with God from a very honest place. When he was confused, he asked questions. When he didn't understand, he rehearsed the character of God. And the result was that he was able to carry on for forty years proclaiming a message almost no one embraced. He started telling God all his real feelings and doubts but then found reassurance and peace as he recalled God' character and might. We all can learn from Jeremiah's example.

When God asks me to do things I don't want to do—such as confront people, take bold steps that could be misunderstood, or write Bible studies on difficult topics—I usually resist at first. But when I finish arguing with God and making excuses, I'm then able to do the things Jeremiah did: rehearse God's character, ask honest questions, and wait on God's response. Only then am I able to surrender to God's voice; and when I do, I have a peace in my soul that literally feels like a weight has been lifted. I smile when I should frown. I experience God holding me together when I should be falling apart. All because I allowed God to confirm His message to me.

It's true for each us: we can count on God to confirm His voice as we honestly wrestle with Him and rehearse His character and Word to combat our conflicted emotions. And the result when we follow God's leading is His supernatural and abiding peace.

When it comes to confirming God's voice, there is one other important element we need to consider, and it's this: *when God tells us something specific, it should happen.*

I can think of times in my life that I clearly heard God's voice. All four of my children struggle with asthma. Many nights I have sat up listening to them breathe, trying to discern whether to call 911 or wait it out until morning. One particular night my five-year-old daughter had a horrible night exchanging air in her wheezy lungs and also felt an intense pain in her side. By morning I drove to the emergency room, unsure whether something was seriously wrong or this would be just another day of asthma breathing treatments.

After X-rays, blood tests, and a visit from a surgeon, there still were no clear answers; and my "momma radar" told me my lethargic daughter was very ill. Shortly after a CAT scan revealed double pneumonia and a lung full of fluid, her organs began to shut down as she went into septic shock. We later found out that the fluid had been infected with a strep virus that had become more than her body could fight off. However, while doctors rushed around her room hooking her body up to machines and calling out medications and dosages, I stood in the midst of what seemed like a medical TV show episode and heard God speak these words very clearly to me: "She will not die." I thought He said it audibly because it was so clear, and so I looked around at the many doctors and nurses flooding the room to see if they had heard it too. It was unmistakable. For those hours when I should have fallen apart, I felt God's peace and lightness.

When our pastor arrived with my husband, Sean, to pray with us, I was embarrassed that I laughed when Sean tried to warn me that she might not make it through the night. I knew what God had said so clearly and believed it with all my heart. Of course, in the weeks that followed, I allowed myself to worry over her health during much smaller setbacks in her recovery. But in that moment, I definitely heard God's voice, and He confirmed it with a miraculous healing of my daughter.

Other times God's voice has not been so clear. A dear friend of mine was struggling with infertility. I prayed almost every day for her, and when I read Scripture that spoke of the blessing of children, I would write her name in the margin of my Bible. One day I thought I heard God say in my spirit that she would get pregnant. "Do you mean this month, Lord? What are you saying?" I asked. When she didn't get pregnant that month, I wondered if I had heard incorrectly. I was concerned about telling my friend what I thought I had heard and giving her false hope. Several months later she underwent a medical procedure, and thankfully, she now has a beautiful baby boy. She did become pregnant, but not during the month I thought she might. I had heard God's voice but added my own expectations regarding the time line.

So how can we tell if God is speaking to us in that still, small voice as we seek Him in prayer or if we are hearing things we want to hear in order to give ourselves permission to do what we want to do? Did God say our church would grow, or do I just want that to be true? Did God bring that friend to mind because I need to call and check on her, or is that just my crazy brain in overdrive? Does God want me to buy these things, or does He have a different plan for this money He has entrusted to me?

In Jeremiah 32, God gives us an example of one way we can know we are on the right track. God told Jeremiah his cousin would come, *and he did*. The Lord offered proof that His words would come true. God said that confirmation would come through the events He prophesied through Jeremiah actually happening—*and they did*.

God wanted the people to know that even though He was going to allow them to suffer, there was still hope for future generations. His desire was not for them to be destroyed but for them to turn from their sin. God's message for His people was hope through surrender. One day God would bring the people back, and they would buy and sell houses again. And the proof would be that what God had said would come to pass.

Many voices shout at us that they have the words of God. But without fail, whenever people claim they have heard God say something, it should happen. We can be confident that when God says something will happen, it does—100 percent of the time.

As followers of Christ there are some messages we don't have to question. We don't have to walk into a store and say, "God, should I steal today?" He has given us His Word with directions and examples for how to live. The message of His gospel does not have to be questioned—God's love, humanity's sin, Christ's death on the cross, and our need to receive Christ personally are clear through Scripture (read Romans for a non-CliffsNotes version). Our commission to tell others the good news is also clear. Yet we need the Spirit's clear leading on how and when to invest in others to be able to share that message.

So here's the bottom line for me and for you: as we listen to God's voice about how we should spend our time, what job we should take, whether we should have another baby, what ministry He is calling us to, or what kind of education is right for our children, we need to look for God to confirm His messages in our lives. Most often in my own life, God uses His Word to bring confirmation, whether that word comes in a sermon, through a friend, or in my personal daily readings; regardless of the source, it is always too clear to be a coincidence. Other times God uses circumstances to confirm His Word—such as when my daughter was healed from septic shock, revealing the truth of God's promise; or the time when time my husband and I heard God say He would provide for a need, and we received a gift for the exact amount the next day. Our God loves to show Himself real to us as we listen for His voice; and when we seek Him for confirmation, we will find Him faithful.

In whatever areas of life we need answers, we can ask God to give us a clear leading. We can bring Him all our questions and complaints and then rehearse back to ourselves what we know to be true about Him. If we will do this, asking God to give us the mercy of confirmation so that we can know we're on the right track of obedience,

He will be faithful to respond. But we must stay close to Him if we are to know His voice.

Learning to discern God's voice and wait for confirmation not only makes us increasingly brave to obey His call but also helps us sort out what success looks like when we obey and things don't look like we thought they would.

Defining Success

In our churches we often measure "success" by how many people attend worship or an event, how many dedicated themselves to Christ in a given period, and how cool and trendy we are as we go about it. Likewise, in our personal lives we often gauge our spiritual success by the ease of our circumstances or the approval of others. We want to see results from the work we do for God. If we don't, then we think we must be doing something wrong. Have you ever thought that?

Of course, we want our lives to have meaning and purpose. God created us with vision, drive, a work ethic, and dreams. These things are not inherently bad. However, we need to evaluate our measuring rod for what constitutes success.

Whether we're aware of it or not, this is where a version of the prosperity gospel sometimes subtly infiltrates our Christian walk. I find this thinking creeping into my own soul at times:

I follow God = everything should go well for me.

But this is not biblical!

The list is long of those who followed God and found hardship and difficulty. Job is a classic example. David lived in caves. Joseph was thrown into a pit and wrongly accused. Jesus ended His ministry with exponentially fewer followers than He had at one time and a gruesome death on a cross. Jeremiah also followed God and encountered difficulty.

Throughout Jeremiah's writings, we see his emotions and some of his thoughts as he struggled to pursue God radically. Jeremiah related his responses to real-life fears and threats with gut-wrenching honesty. He didn't stuff his feelings about what he was going through—and that's a much-needed lesson for many of us "good Christians."

As you evaluate your life, remember that some circumstances are just difficult. God didn't expect Jeremiah to celebrate the sin of his people, death threats, or rumors spread about him. In the same way, He doesn't want you to pretend your own problems are of no consequence. He created you with emotions that respond to circumstances, and it's okay to feel and express them. In fact, it's *necessary*.

Whether it's something small like a teenager not making a sports team or a bigger trial like a health challenge that persists, we have to learn that it is okay to not be okay. When my daughter lost all of her hair to an autoimmune disorder called alopecia at the age of twelve, a well-meaning friend said, "Well, at least she doesn't have cancer." That is true, but it doesn't diminish the emotions that I had in watching my sweet girl grieve the loss of her hair. When we express our feelings to God and others, we bring our pain into the light rather than letting it fester in the darkness.

Jeremiah shows us that even the most faithful followers can feel anxiety and depression and struggle to believe God through rough circumstances. These struggles do not mean we are unsuccessful Christians. Instead, they give us an opportunity to take our thoughts and emotions to God, who always invites us to come to Him and wrestle through our personal battles. We must resist the urge to numb ourselves with food, television, social media, and any other distraction that keeps us from dealing with our pain and, instead, take it to the Lord. I know, I know—*this can be hard*! It's so easy to reach for the remote, cell phone, or refrigerator door. That's why we need prayer, God's Word, Christian community, and sometimes a good counselor to help us sort out the very real trials that ravage our lives.

Our trials are often seasonal and temporary. However, Jeremiah's ministry did not have a silver lining like the stories of some other Bible heroes. David lived in caves but eventually was crowned king. Joseph labored in prison but was elevated to second-in-command over all Egypt. Jeremiah, on the other hand, is called the weeping prophet because the message God gave him was difficult. It wasn't fun to deliver, and people didn't listen.

Jeremiah was imprisoned, mocked, put in a cistern, and eventually taken to Egypt against his will. Though he wasn't left in that cistern, he didn't end up on top with a great life after just a few years of difficulty. He may have seemed unsuccessful according to the world's standards, and yet in God's economy he was very accomplished. He lived for God's kingdom, followed God's instructions, and stayed true to the words God gave Him to speak. To put it simply, Jeremiah was a success in God's eyes because he was faithful and obedient. In eternity he can look back on his rough road in life knowing that he lived it well even though it wasn't easy.

Jeremiah's story gives us great hope for our own struggles. In our culture we tend to want instant gratification and to measure success by immediate results. Did it "work"? What do people think? Do my kids behave, get good grades, and excel in sports? Are others impressed with my nice home? Do I have enough status in my job? When will I get a promotion? These are the outward measures of doing it right today. But God's standards of success are not the same as ours. We might follow God wholeheartedly and still lose our job, get sick, or face financial ruin. We may not look to others like the greatest now, but God says that those who sacrifice their wills for His will be great in heaven.

The world says "blessed are those who are rich, happy, proud, selfish, self-indulgent, critical, promiscuous, demanding, and rewarded." But Jesus says "blessed are the pure" (Matthew 5:8 NIV). The world says to mix in a little "bad girl" or "bad boy." Yet God's standards starkly contrast what the world labels as desirable. He blesses those who are poor, sorrowful, humble, and hungry for what is right, merciful, pure, peaceable, and persecuted.

Here is a sure truth to grab hold of when we are lost in the lies of this world:

> *Even though God allows us to experience trials, He promises to be with us and take care of us through them.*

Though Jeremiah's life was difficult, it was also truly blessed. He was surrendered to God's call. He based his success on his obedience, not on any temporary circumstances. He was also super honest with God about his feelings, pain, uncertainty, and even despair. When surrender gives us anxiety, Jeremiah shows us that we can bring all of it to God.

Dealing with White Flag Anxiety

I felt sick to my stomach with fear and anxiety. I had just found out that the school district where our church and four other church plants hold services was doubling the rental rates. This came at the same time when support from our sending church ended and offerings were down. I was freaking out. *Where does a church planter's wife go to resign?* I wondered. Can you quit a job that has no monetary compensation?

Then, as I lay on my face asking God what He was doing, He told me to think about what I was writing at the time—a Bible study on the life of Jeremiah. Jeremiah faced one difficult situation after another. He struggled with depression. He was left in a cistern to die. He knew that according to God's messages, the people of Israel were facing seventy years of captivity. Yet in the midst of it all he clung to the Lord, trusting in God to take care of him.

Jeremiah didn't try to sugarcoat his pain but boldly told God that he wished he were never born. He actually called God's help uncertain and blamed Him for the suffering he endured. You might say that Jeremiah held nothing back.

Our lives are often like Jeremiah's, with circumstances that range anywhere from puzzling to downright depressing. At times we all find ourselves saying things like "I'm done!" or "I give up!" But we can know with confidence that God is the One who will take care of us. Rather than leave us as orphans in a sea of questions, trials, and difficulties, God promises to walk with us just as He did with Jeremiah.

Let's take a look at two active steps Jeremiah took as he brought his complaints to God. We find them in Jeremiah 15:16-17. The first thing Jeremiah did was devour God's Word. Though he didn't have access to the entire biblical canon that we are privileged to possess in great abundance—even having the entire Bible in multiple translations on our phones—we know he came in contact with the Pentateuch, the first five books of the Bible. How do we know that these scrolls, which were rediscovered by King Josiah early in Jeremiah's ministry, influenced the prophet?

For one thing, the prophets Isaiah and Hosea wrote one hundred years before Jeremiah began to dictate his messages from God to the scribe named Baruch, yet we see glimpses of their influence on Jeremiah in his messages. Also, word pictures from the psalmists echo into the pages of his prophecy. The evidence is unmistakable: Jeremiah devoured God's inspired words like food. And he didn't consume God's Word accidentally; it was an intentional act of his will, not his emotions. (After all, his emotions were much like ours—flittering from despair to hope from one moment to another.) Jeremiah set his will to study God's Word, and his emotions followed truth as he argued and experienced the living Word.

The second practical step Jeremiah took was to stand alone. Jeremiahs 15:17 says he chose the unpopular route of nonconformity. God responded by clearly calling Jeremiah with a powerful passage:

> "If you return to me, I will restore you
> so you can continue to serve me.
> If you speak good words rather than worthless ones,
> you will be my spokesman.
> You must influence them;
> do not let them influence you!"
> (Jeremiah 15:19)

I don't know about you, but I'd like to inscribe this verse on some of my children's belongings. For that matter, I need to carry it with me as well!

Though translators have used words like *return*, *turn*, and

We should be people who draw others to our God rather than people who are pulled away from Him by our culture.

influence when translating this verse, the Hebrew word used here is *shuwb*. It means "to turn back, to lead away."[3] We should be people who draw others to our God rather than people who are pulled away from Him by our culture. God called Jeremiah to be the influencer, and we, too, are called to be influencers in a world where we're continually surrounded by all kinds of stimuli. In a world full of screens that have a constant flow of information and entertainment, God calls us to set an example rather than embrace the status quo.

In order to be the influencer instead of the influenced, Jeremiah devoured God's Word and chose to stand alone. We must do the same if we want to be able to stand for God in our culture. The truth is that the tendency to fall in with the crowd didn't end in middle school for any of us. I have to confess that I have joined in with the crowd regarding media choices, gossip, spending habits, and other areas of life where taking a stand could be unpopular. I've also been dragged down instead of being a spokeswoman with God's message. What about you? Have you ever found it easier to get sucked into the habits of those around you when it comes to your time, thought life, and media choices? Where is God calling you to be His spokesperson in not just what you say but also how you live?

It can be hard to stand alone—it might even give us some anxiety and internal struggle. But God is a safe place. We can trust Him with our fears, our anxiety, our wins, and our losses. He is our refuge.

Making God Our Safe Place

What does it mean to say that God is our refuge or safe place? Every trial, frustration, and battle with flesh and sin that leaves us ready to call it quits fades in comparison with the blessing that comes from fully yielding to our God. He paints a picture so that His people won't miss the joy of a life fully yielded to His message. In fact, God so desperately doesn't want us to miss this truth about His protection and care for us in the midst of life's trials that He gives us two visuals.

The first picture, found in Jeremiah 17:5-8, is the dry shrub for those who trust in human strength:

> This is what the LORD says:
> "Cursed are those who put their trust in mere humans,
>   who rely on human strength
>   and turn their hearts away from the
>   LORD.
> They are like stunted shrubs in the desert,
>   with no hope for the future.
> They will live in the barren wilderness,
>   in an uninhabited salty land.
>
> "But blessed are those who trust in the LORD
>   and have made the LORD their hope and
>   confidence.
> They are like trees planted along a riverbank,
>   with roots that reach deep into the water.
> Such trees are not bothered by the heat
>   or worried by long months of drought.
> Their leaves stay green,
>   and they never stop producing fruit.

The Hebrew word for trust in this passage is *batach*, which actually means "a place of refuge" or "safe place."[4] When we make people or anything wrought of human effort our safe place, God lets us know what we have to look forward to—and it's not pretty. The people in Jeremiah's day chose to trust in political alliances and idolatry. They lost faith in the God of their ancestors. They even looked to Egypt for help—the same country that held them captive as slaves for over four hundred years in the days of Moses. God called them to trust Him, letting them know clearly what the results of human help would be.

In His Word God doesn't leave us to wonder what will happen if we make our safe place the government, our jobs, our friendships, or even our families. People die, children grow up, and regimes change. God tells us that we will find ourselves in the condition of being unproductive, hopeless, isolated, and bitter if we place our ultimate trust in anything but Him alone. He says that we will live in a barren wilderness, an uninhabited salty land. God graciously will do whatever it takes to "wake us up" from this state—just as He allowed the people of Judah to face destruction and captivity in order to help them see their "barrenness" and how far they had drifted from Him.

God also gives us a picture of the other alternative, telling us that when we trust in Him we will be stable, nourished, vibrant, and productive. Deep roots in Him will make us stable! This blessed life will not be problem-free; God honestly tells us we may still encounter heat and long months of drought. However, we won't dry up because His water from the river will nourish us. He promises to keep our leaves green and still produce fruit in our lives—even in dry times.

What a contrast to the salty shrub is the sweet fruit of the Spirit in our lives, nourishing those around us. When we make the Lord our hope and confidence, we not only will produce fruit but also will get to be part of God's plan for healing in this broken world. Making God our safe place means that He will take care of us *and* use us for His kingdom work; and that's a double blessing.

Jeremiah's life may not have been one of comfort, status, and material wealth; but he had great treasure—blessings to come in the next life as well as blessings to enjoy in his life on earth, even in the midst of trials. I don't know about you, but this speaks to my soul! The blessed life is far better than the circumstantially happy life because it is not dependent on anything but the Lord. Only He is unchanging. Only He is secure. Only He can be fully trusted. The most secure of careers can end tomorrow; the most stable family can be quickly interrupted by divorce or tragedy. Whenever we trust in human resources, we are like a shrub in the desert that dries up and dies. But when we make the Lord our confidence, we can weather the times of drought and heat.

Like Jeremiah, we are God's messengers, and He promises to take care of us. He gives us His Word to build our faith and encourage us to trust Him even when it seems like He doesn't care. As a loving Father, He longs to be close to His children. He never forces us to come near, but He calls to us through His Word to put our hope and confidence in Him alone. How will we respond?

Just as Jeremiah brought his complaints and then waited for God to respond, take time to ask God your hard questions. Then listen for His voice; and when He answers you, surrender to that voice with obedience. He will not fail you!

Dare to Hope Challenge

What pulls you away from God? It might be a person, an addiction, an activity, or something you turn to instead of (or before) God. List everything that comes to mind on an index card. These are the idols in your life—those people or things that you have elevated above God. Spend some time in prayer, surrendering your list to God and asking what steps you need to take in order to draw closer to Him. Write these steps on the other side of the card, and post it somewhere you will see it regularly.

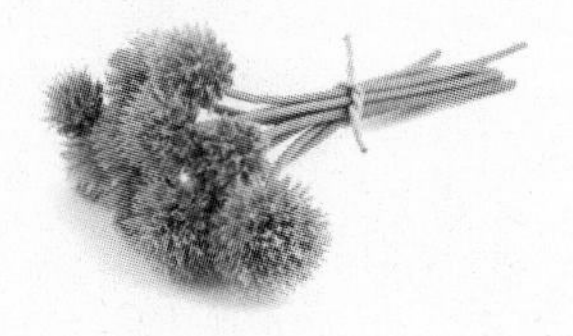

CHAPTER 2

Recognizing Counterfeits and the Real Deal

Reject Counterfeits

Idols are worthless; they are ridiculous lies!
On the day of reckoning they will all be destroyed.
But the God of Israel is no idol!
He is the Creator of everything that exists,
including Israel, his own special possession.
The Lord of Heaven's Armies is his name!
—Jeremiah 10:15-16

The feeling of having forgotten something important is no fun. For ten years, I unlocked the door and checked people in for a 6:00 a.m. exercise class two days a week. This meant I had to get up at 5:30 a.m. to get there in time. (Yes, I often slept in my workout clothes and rolled out of bed, brushed my teeth, grabbed a water bottle, and jumped in my car.) I love the other crazy girls that got up early to get a workout finished before it's light outside. A few times I had gotten my days mixed up or not set my alarm correctly. When I woke up and realized that I'd overslept and missed my commitment, it started my whole day off on the wrong note. I'd let others down. I had forgotten something I was supposed to remember. A friend of mine placed a sticky note right on her steering wheel to help her remember her car-pool schedule. Too many times she had forgotten, and she hated the feeling of not getting it right.

What is something you sometimes forget?

Over twenty-five times the words *remind*, *remember*, *forget*, or *forgotten* are used in the Book of Jeremiah. God knows our tendency to forget and calls us to intentionally set patterns in our lives to help us remember Him against the backdrop of counterfeit gods screaming for our attention—and there's no shortage of those in our culture!

While I needed to remember to get my sleepy self out of bed in time for my exercise class, and my friend needed to know when to pick up extra children in the carpool, and you may need to remember a deadline or an event or some other responsibility, the people of Judah forgot something of much greater magnitude. Their forgetfulness carried intense consequences.

God's powerful hand that brought the Israelites out of slavery in Egypt also wrote His sacred instructions on tablets of stone. The second commandment on that list of the big ten contains the most detailed explanation of them all:

> "You must not make for yourself an idol of any kind or an image of anything in the heavens or on the earth or in the sea. You must not bow down to them or worship them, for I, the LORD your God, am a jealous God who will not tolerate your affection for any other gods. I lay the sins of the parents upon their children; the entire family is affected—even children in the third and fourth generations of those who reject me. But I lavish unfailing love for a thousand generations on those who love me and obey my commands." (Exodus 20:4-6)

Idolatry is no laughing matter for God. He will not share affection with other gods, and He knows that counterfeits can be shiny and attractive. In Exodus 23:33, the phrase "caught in the trap of idolatry" describes the predicament of allowing our hearts to lean toward false gods. Some versions of Scripture call idolatry a trap, and others say it's a snare. God warns His people that the things of this world will try to lure them away. Like the Sirens in Greek mythology who sang beautiful songs to lure men to their death, so this world sings lies to us that our God is not enough. The bait looks dangerously similar to the real thing so that we will fall for the counterfeit. I've been guilty of listening to the "music" and taking the bait, and I'm sure you have too. The people in Jeremiah's day were no different. That's why Jeremiah called them to remember their God—because they were trapped in the sin of idolatry and couldn't see the rot in their souls.

Early in Jeremiah's ministry a short-lived revival had occurred when King Josiah had discovered scrolls containing God's laws during Temple repairs. Though scholars disagree as to exactly which Bible books the scrolls contained, we learn from 2 Kings 22 that during King Josiah's reign reforms were enacted based on a reading of God's words about His strict forbiddance of idolatry. Shortly after this renewal of faith and turning away from idolatry, however, the people quickly fell back into their old patterns of sin.

Unfortunately, that's often our story as well. We are a people who are prone to forget God.

Remembering God

It seems absurd that we could forget God, and yet we do it with regularity. The prophet Jeremiah wrote about the absurdity of forgetting God by likening it to a bride not remembering her wedding dress or a young woman forgetting her jewelry (Jeremiah 2:32). It's a powerful analogy. I remember staring at my ring during college classes after I got engaged. I could barely concentrate on what my professors were saying about history of doctrine, Western civilization, or even systematic theology with that brilliant thing glowing up at me. I had never worn a ring or much jewelry at all before my future husband offered me a beautiful diamond when he asked me to marry him. Dreaming of a life with him and the hope of what the future held for us sparkled in that band around my finger. You can bet I never forgot about my jewelry then! And how many brides forget where they have put their wedding gowns? No, we take great care with these items because they are important to us.

If we're honest, we all could say that we are forgetful at times when it comes to our affection for God. Sometimes we are more careful with our clothing, cell phones, and workout regimens than with our relationship with the living God. We can take greater care to eat right and exercise than to keep our hearts right with our Creator. But thankfully, we do not have to worry that our God will ever forget about *us*. He will always, always, always remember us.

In Jeremiah 11 we see that God called His people to remember His *covenant* with them. This is a word that has escaped our vernacular. Covenants in our culture remind us of marriage ceremonies in which a man and woman make a covenant to love each other forever. In a world where more than 50 percent of these vows will not stand the test of time, it is difficult to wrap our minds around what God is saying; but He is not like us. Our God is a promise-keeper. When He says to worship Him alone, He means it. When He says there will be consequences if we don't, He isn't taking it lightly. God wanted the people to remember the covenant they had made with Him. So He pointed out their idolatry, calling it "altars of shame" (11:13).

Our faithful, covenant-keeping God is the One who created us, the One who sees the master plan, and the One who desires a close relationship with us despite our own unfaithfulness. Regrettably, the things of this earth that urgently cry out for our attention often relegate God to the bottom of the list. If we call ourselves Christ-followers, our relationship with God should be the number one thing in our lives; yet so often we forget what is most important because of the lure of things of this world.

This is not a new problem. Even without television, magazines, the internet, and other modern media, the people of Israel were so focused on the things of this earth that they forgot their God. Jeremiah was God's prophet calling out to the people: "Don't forget God because you are so focused on things you can touch, taste, and feel." This message was so important that we read it again and again throughout the Book of Jeremiah. In fact, over forty verses scattered throughout the book mention idols. We can read these verses and self-righteously accuse the Israelites. They got caught making things with their own hands and worshipping them instead of God. They participated in adultery, lust, and child sacrifice and spent their time and money pouring out offerings to imaginary gods. But the truth is that although our idolatry may look different, the same root lies beneath the surface of our actions.

Our hearts can be drawn in so many directions today. Our phones, our social media persona, our desire for the next rung on the ladder of success, whatever that looks like—these are just some of the idols that can steal our affection from God. I'm sure you can think of others. While our idols may not be physical statues and our worship may not include pouring out drinks or burning incense to them, God calls us to keep Him foremost in our lives. And still our hearts often succumb to our culture's more subtle relationship with idolatry.

An idol is anything we might worship other than God, yet in our culture the very word *idol* has taken on a harmless connotation—such as with the long-running television show *American Idol.* In the context of the show, an idol is something to be adored or appreciated. Now, most of us have never worshipped the contestants on *American Idol* but merely have enjoyed their God-given talent. Even so, we can set up idols just as easily as the Israelites in Jeremiah's day when we spend more time and effort focusing on anything other than God. Just as God asked the people of Judah to remember Him, He asks the same thing of us. He made a new covenant with us through the blood of His Son, Jesus, and He wants us to remember what He has done—to remember Him.

So many other things are calling out for your time and attention. Don't let the minutia of life crowd out the most important thing: your relationship with your Creator. Put a sticky note on your steering wheel with a Scripture verse or a reminder to pray, set an alarm to signal your devotional time, let your church attendance or small group take priority over your sports commitments. Do whatever it takes to remember the covenant you made the day you asked Christ to take first place in your life. If we aren't intentional, counterfeits will replace God's best for us, and they never really satisfy.

Spotting a Fake

One of the best ways to guard against a counterfeit is to learn to spot a fake.

I remember being at church camp as a teenager and hearing the speaker tell a story of a little girl with a fake pearl necklace. Here is my version of this popular and often-told story. A little girl bought a plastic pearl necklace with the money she had been saving all year. She loved her pearls and felt so grown up when she wore them. She only took them off when she went swimming or took a bath. Though the pearls weren't real, that didn't matter to her. She had bought them all by herself.

This little girl had a loving father. One day he said to her, "Honey, do you love me?"

"Yes, Daddy," she said. "You know I love you."

"Then will you give me your pearls?" her father asked.

"Not my pearls!" the little girl practically gasped. "But you can have my toy horse."

"That's okay, Sweetheart. I love you," he replied. And then he kissed her cheek. About a week later, the father asked his little girl again, "Do you love me?"

"Daddy, you know I love you," she said.

"Then will you give me your pearls?" he repeated.

"Not my pearls. But I'll give you my baby doll."

"That's okay. I love you," the father answered. And once again he gave her a kiss on the cheek.

This same routine happened again and again, and the little girl began to wonder, "If Daddy loves me, why does he want to take away something I love?"

Then one day the little girl walked up to her father with tears in her eyes and held out her fake pearl necklace. "Here, Daddy. This is for you," she said.

The father reached out a hand to take the necklace, and with his other hand he reached into his pocket and pulled out a velvet case. Inside that case was a strand of genuine pearls, chosen with love and care for his daughter. He had had the pearls all along but was waiting for his daughter to give up what she had so that he could give her something even better.

As we read God's strong reaction to idolatry in Jeremiah, let's not forget His heart behind it. He sees us settling for a fake when He wants to give us the real thing—and we're not talking about a necklace. The stakes are much higher; they echo into eternity.

The second chapter of Jeremiah lays out clearly God's heart regarding idolatry:

> This is what the Lord says:
>
> "What did your ancestors find wrong with me
> that led them to stray so far from me?
> They worshiped worthless idols,
> only to become worthless themselves.
> They did not ask, 'Where is the Lord
> who brought us safely out of Egypt
> and led us through the barren wilderness…'
>
> "Go west and look in the land of Cyprus;
> go east and search through the land of Kedar.
> Has anyone ever heard of anything
> as strange as this?
> Has any nation ever traded its gods for new ones,
> even though they are not gods at all?
> Yet my people have exchanged their glorious God
> for worthless idols!
> The heavens are shocked at such a thing
> and shrink back in horror and dismay,"
> says the Lord.

"For my people have done two evil things:
They have abandoned me—
the fountain of living water.
And they have dug for themselves cracked cisterns
that can hold no water at all!"

(Jeremiah 2:5-6, 10-13)

Idolatry's precursor is forgetfulness. When we neglect to remember all the ways God has shown Himself in our lives, we make ourselves easy prey for the world's counterfeit offerings. In these verses God warns His people to ask, "Where is the Lord?" We, too, can become apathetic when our circumstances overwhelm us, turning to people, money, and human wisdom to try to make sense of our problems. I know I've been there. How about you?

The fountain of living water and the cracked cisterns are one of the many great physical illustrations God gives to help us understand what happens when we trust in the things we can see and feel instead of yielding ourselves to Him. Like in the story of the fake pearls, we tend to hold tightly to what we think will help us through. We put our trust in people, jobs, status, money, and any number of things that may seem safer to trust than God. We dig in our heels with empty systems that aren't really secure and make our own feeble attempts at feeling safe and loved. But it's all just a cracked cistern—and a cracked cistern is *leaky*! It's probably filled with sludge and dirty water like the cistern Jeremiah was lowered into. Yet because it's tangible, we'll settle for it over the fountain of living water.

Cracked cisterns aren't just damaged; they are completely useless. In order to identify the cracked cisterns in our lives, we need a modern definition of idolatry. Timothy Keller, author of *Counterfeit Gods*, defines an idol as "anything more important to you than God, anything that absorbs your heart and imagination more than God, anything you seek to give you what only God can give."[1] This idolatry can take two forms:

1. an inherently bad object, practice, or habit; or
2. a good person, thing, or practice that we elevate above God.

Some counterfeits are not necessarily bad things in and of themselves. Yet anything that we elevate above God—including relationships, careers, hobbies, or possessions—can become an idol in our lives. One idol I have long battled is productivity. I want to do measurable things all the time so that I feel a sense of accomplishment. Sometimes I will write an item on my to-do list after I've already done it just so that I can cross it off. God is teaching me to rest and be still so I can be close to Him instead of feeling the need to constantly accomplish something.

I love these tender words about idolatry in 1 John 5:21, "Dear children, keep away from anything that might take God's place in your hearts." If your idol is an important person or persons in your life such as a husband or children, then obviously you can't "stay away" from them (though on some days you probably should—not only for your sake but for theirs!). However, there are some things we just need to make a clean break from. Period.

Here's an exercise that may sound silly but has been very effective for me. I remember throwing a stick representing a bad habit or sin into a fire at church camp and writing sins on pieces of paper and throwing them in a fire at youth group. I have forgotten the specifics of most of the Bible lessons taught me during my childhood and teenage years, but these times of watching a stick or paper burn have stuck in my mind. They were marked moments when I asked God to light a fire in me. Though there were later struggles and relapses in the areas I had identified, those moments began a journey toward freedom for me.

Is there a practice, habit, harmful relationship, media choice, or secret sin that God is calling you to turn your back on in order to keep Him first in your heart? I encourage you to write it on a piece of paper, surrender it to God, and then burn it with a lighter or match. (I'm not kidding. Actually do it—preferably in a kitchen sink or outside.) Then ask God to help you remember the flame of your own paper burning and get started on the road to freedom in this area that you identified. Make it a moment you will never forget, the moment you started a real fire both literally and spiritually!

Now, when idols are good things, it's a little trickier to know how to remove them. Sometimes idols can be things such as children, spouses, or romantic relationships, or intangible things such as our appearance, comfort, security, or ability to bring order to our lives (which is a nice way of saying control!). Idols also can be time-suckers in our lives such as TV, social media, or romance novels. There is no end to the list of things that can take God's place in our hearts.

Something crosses the line into idolatry based on its elevation in our heart and mind. Our loving God has given us our families, jobs, and ministries as gifts, but the danger comes when these things become ultimate or deified. If we lose them, we will feel great sorrow; but will we *despair*? If the loss of our status, money, or family member will reduce us to unrelenting despair, then that person or thing may have begun to take the place of God in our hearts and become an idol.

In *Counterfeit Gods*, Timothy Keller helps us see just how we elevate things above God:

> We know a good thing has become a counterfeit god when its demands on you exceed proper boundaries. Making an idol out of work may mean that you work until you ruin your health, or you break the laws in order to get ahead. Making an idol out of love may mean allowing the lover to exploit and abuse you, or it may cause terrible blindness to the pathologies in the relationship. An idolatrous attachment can lead you to break any promise, rationalize any indiscretion, or betray any other allegiance, in order to hold on to it. It may drive you to violate all good and proper boundaries. To practice idolatry is to be a slave.[2]

A slave. That really gets our attention, doesn't it?

In chapter 2 of Jeremiah, we see that God is frustrated that the people would not admit their sin. They didn't recognize that they were slaves to it. Of course, He already knew about it, just as He knows about our own struggles with idol worship. But here's the good news: we only need to confess these idols and ask Him to help us walk in repentance. And when we do—when we release and surrender what we're holding too tightly, like the fake pearls the little girl clenched in her hand—then God can give us the real thing: Himself.

On the pages of Scripture it seems so clear, but in the real world it's not so easy. How will we pay the bills? Who will be a loyal friend? Who will help me with a difficult boss? Will I really survive motherhood? Can we trust God to be the fountain, or should we dig a cistern on the side just to be sure?

Timothy Keller offers another helpful observation:

> Here, then, is the practical answer to our own idolatries, . . . which are not spiritually safe to have and hold. We need to offer them up. We need to find a way to keep from clutching them too tightly, of being enslaved to them. We will never do so by mouthing abstractions about how great God is. We have to know, to be assured, that God so loves, cherishes, and delights in us that we can rest our hearts in him for our significance and security and handle anything that happens in life.[3]

Only when we embrace God as the fountain of living water are we able to stop trusting in our cracked cisterns. In order to identify and smash our idols, we must realize God wants to give us the real thing. The cracked cistern doesn't even begin to compare with the fountain God offers, and God has not changed His mind on this topic. When we elevate people, stuff, status, or anything our culture promotes for fulfillment, we exchange our glorious God for counterfeits. It's heartbreaking, really.

God uses the illustration of the fountain and the cracked cistern in Jeremiah 2, but by chapter 51 He cuts to the chase and uses the strongest possible language:

> The whole human race is foolish and has no knowledge!
> The craftsmen are disgraced by the idols
> they make,
> for their carefully shaped works are a fraud.
> These idols have no breath or power.
> Idols are worthless; they are ridiculous lies!
> On the day of reckoning they will all be destroyed.
> But the God of Israel is no idol!

> He is the Creator of everything that exists,
> including his people, his own special possession.
> The LORD of Heaven's Armies is his name!
> (Jeremiah 51:17-19)

Could it be any clearer? If we're going to stop our apathetic satisfaction with substitutes, we must find satisfaction in the true Creator God. He alone truly is satisfying. He alone offers the real deal. And here's the best part: when we let go of our idols, we experience the thrill of real peace *down deep*—the kind that isn't dependent on other people, circumstances, or things.

God's pearls are priceless—no cheap imitations. I dare you to loosen your grip on the fakes and give God a chance to satisfy your soul with His Spirit, His Word, Himself. Try it and see! You'll find that the result is all the fullness of life with God. If you don't—if you refuse to loosen your grip on lesser things—then it's only a matter of time until you experience the inevitable consequences of counterfeits.

Counterfeit Consequences

Disciplining my four children has never been a joy to me. At times I wanted to ignore disobedience or bad behavior because I just didn't want to deal with it. Yet I understood the truth of Proverbs 13:24b, "Those who love their children care enough to discipline them." I remember a particular Friday Family Fun Night (which we had often at the Spoelstra house during the elementary school years) when we were all watching a movie together, and one of our children had to stay in her bedroom because she disobeyed even after clear warnings about the possible consequences. It broke my heart, but I knew she needed to feel the sting of her decision.

Like a loving Parent, God tried to correct His people's disobedient and harmful ways by sending His prophets to share His messages. These prophets reminded the people of their history and God's laws. When they refused to listen and chose to keep making their own gods, God gave them consequences so that they would stop allowing the things they could touch and feel to replace the real God who had created and loved them. God was willing to stop these consequences if they would stop their idolatrous ways, but they persisted. Eventually, after their continual disobedience, God's patience waned.

God had given opportunity after opportunity for the people to stop their idol worship and turn back to Him. You can hear the loving heart of God in these verses, pleading with them to turn from their evil ways: "But I will be merciful only if you stop your evil thoughts and deeds and start treating each other with justice; only if you stop exploiting foreigners, orphans, and widows; only if you stop your murdering; and only if you stop harming yourselves by worshipping idols. Then I will let you stay in this land that I gave to your ancestors to keep forever" (Jeremiah 7:5-7).

Just as good parents can't stand to see their children make bad choices that lead to pain, God does not want His children to make choices that bring them harm. He is the perfect parent, and He clearly lays out His expectations through His Word. However, when He sees His people continually making self-destructive choices, He steps in to draw them back to the right path. He will go to any length to help them, which includes discipline. Eventually, God would destroy their land because of their ongoing disobedience.

Just as our idolatry takes a different form today, the consequences of our idolatry also take shape differently in our culture. The crops

As we realize the ramifications of our personal idolatry and take steps of obedience toward God, it causes a ripple effect to those in our spheres of influence.

and land might not be consumed in front of our eyes, but when our hearts are consumed with lesser gods, we don't have space for the good things of the Living God—peace, joy, wholeness, grace, mercy, hope. Our consequences might come in the form of apathy, lack of contentment, and stress.

Here's the good news: it takes only one glance toward God, and away from lesser idols, to start the journey of repentance. When we begin to stare intently at God by talking to Him, listening to His Word, and gathering with His people, we will find that we don't need to stare so much at lesser things.

What's true for us personally is also true for us collectively. Cultures change one person at a time, so the first step in turning the tide of our nation starts with a look in the mirror. The only person I can truly change is me, and the only person you can truly change is you. As we realize the ramifications of our personal idolatry and take steps of obedience toward God, it causes a ripple effect to those in our spheres of influence—our family members, friends, neighbors, coworkers, and others. Then as we continue to forsake idols and let God take first place in our lives, those around us may be inspired to make their own changes and affect those in *their* spheres of influence. This is where Jesus started: one person at a time.

Now, let us take this one step closer to home and consider how our personal idolatry grieves the heart of God. Remember Tim Keller's words, "To practice idolatry is to be a slave"? Our idolatry grieves God so intensely because it leads us needlessly into slavery. God sent His Son to purchase our freedom at a very high cost. Watching us live enslaved to idols must be similar to loving parents watching their drug-addicted child ruin his or her life.

As I have parented my four children—three who are now in

college and one who is still in high school—I've often had to enforce painful consequences. When my kids have chosen to go their own way and have made choices contrary to the rules we have set for their safety and well-being, it has grieved my heart. Their disregard for siblings, their lack of trustworthiness when we've discovered they have lied, and their decisions that have threatened their personal safety have even caused anger in me because of my great love and concern for them. Of course, I desperately want them to make decisions that will lead to their ultimate protection and success. So when I've found out that they've lied to me, it has hurt and angered me at the same time. I want to trust them, and these acts of disobedience have set our relationship back and brought consequences into their lives.

In the same way, I believe God feels heartbreak and perhaps even righteous anger when we sin, not because of His lack of love but because He desires our good and knows how our disobedience causes setbacks in our relationship with Him. We find the theme of God's intense reaction to idolatry throughout the pages of Jeremiah. Why? Because God wants what is best for His children. In fact, God is so loving and gracious that He sent His own Son to die for our sins. He doesn't want anything to stand in the way of our ultimate good. This is why He desires to be first in our lives—because this is what is best for us. He does not want to play second fiddle to anything or anyone because He knows that will separate us from Him.

Though it is right to emphasize God's great love and grace, we must not forget His justice—His righteous anger toward sin that, left unchecked, would destroy us. In fact, it is that righteous anger toward sin that makes His extravagant grace so amazing. By sending His one and only Son to die for our sins, He made a way for us to be redeemed and reconciled to Him. So when we continue to live in idolatry, we cheapen His incredible sacrifice. He bought our freedom at a great price. Why, then, do we continue to choose slavery?

Over and over God warns us about idolatry, but the people of Jeremiah's day wouldn't listen. They had access to the law of Moses as well as God's messengers proclaiming His word. Yet they couldn't see God. They didn't see immediate consequences. Sometimes it's no different for me and you.

Have you ever continued in sin because it seems you're "getting away" without punishment? Me too. What I don't always realize is that even when I don't see immediate results of my personal idolatry, the apathy in my spirit, the missed opportunities, and the ultimate consequences on my relationships do affect me. Every time.

God does not take idolatry lightly. He is jealous over our relationship with Him, which is a way of saying that He desires unhindered intimacy with us. Just as we love our children enough to give them consequences, so our heavenly Father is willing to discipline us. Yes, we are under the new covenant now. We have Christ's sacrifice as the payment for our sins. However, God still wants us to put away our idols and worship Him because this is what leads to our wholeness and peace. And deep down, that's really what we want too.

But let's be honest. Sometimes we can be so busy with all the details of work, family, school, sports, and hobbies that we stumble in the door at the end of the day and just want to escape. We turn on the TV or computer or turn to food or some other empty habit because it seems like a "quick fix." Then we justify our bad habits, consumer attitudes, selfishness—aka our idols—just as the people of Israel did. Oh, that we would learn our lessons without having to endure the heavy consequences as they did! Just as I want the wholeness that comes from a right relationship with God for each of my children, this is what God wants for each of us.

Romans 8:1 tells us "there is no condemnation for those who belong to Christ Jesus," and this is good news. No, it's *great* news! In His goodness and grace, God makes us aware of our sin and asks us to turn from it. God takes our sin seriously and, because He is a good Father, desperately wants us to obey His Word. He is jealous for you and for me because He loves us so deeply. Not only that, He never gives up on us! *Never.*

Despite what some of us may have believed, it is never too late to return to God. In Jeremiah 7:3, God says, "Even now, if you quit your evil ways, I will let you stay in your own land." In other words, He would preserve and protect His people. God says the same thing to us today. "Even now" we can turn away from counterfeits and run straight into His arms—the safest place to be.

What a joy it is to know that we can always return to God, no matter the mess we've made or how far we've run from Him. Counterfeit idols can be super shiny and enticing, stealing our affection before we even realize it. In Jeremiah's day and in our own, money, greed, and wealth are counterfeits that promise power and the perfect life. But the irony is that the more resources we have, the more we need to pay attention to our heart's one true desire; because stuff never satisfies.

Settling for Stuff

I'm just going to admit it. I am a Dave Ramsey junkie. My husband, Sean, would call him "the other man in my life." Sometimes when I would be at home during the day and talk to Sean on the phone, he would hear someone in the background and say, "What's

What a joy it is to know that we can always return to God, no matter the mess we've made or how far we've run from Him.

Dave got to say today?" I downloaded his podcasts, and they entertained me while I did chores around the house. I'm not sure why I am so intrigued by the money problems and successes of the callers. But what I learned listening to *The Dave Ramsey Show* is that many of us in the United States, who have so much more than the rest of the world, don't have a clue where all the money has gone at the end of every month. Has that ever happened to you?

Jeremiah has plenty to teach us about "what not to do" in our attitudes and actions toward money—just as Stacy and Clinton kept us from fashion faux pas on the television show *What Not to Wear*. Do you remember that show from several years ago? On the show a real-life person was caught with a wardrobe of sloppy or ill-fitting clothes and had to bring their entire closet to be critiqued. After they discovered what they were doing wrong, Stacy and Clinton would coach them on what they should be looking for so they could dress for their body type and lifestyle. I enjoyed watching and learning since I often found myself living in mom jeans and T-shirts during that season of my life. We might say that Jeremiah cleans out the closet of money myths.

Let's start with the first issue God repeated continually. He was very concerned about Judah's sins of omission—in other words, sins of neglect. The people were greedy and overlooked those who couldn't take care of themselves. The orphans, poor, foreigners, widows, and innocents lived in poverty while the rest of the country got rich and thought only of their own luxury. In our affluent culture we might be tempted to gloss over this issue, but we cannot take it too lightly. Serving those who cannot care for themselves is not a box to be checked off on our "Christian duty" list. It is the essence of what it means to know God.

God says that how we treat others reveals something about our love for Him. If we know Him and walk closely with Him, our hearts will align with His to help those with very real, tangible needs. Our compassion will be stirred just as God's is when He hears the cries of His people. James even calls this kind of deep compassion for orphans and widows "pure and genuine religion" to God (James 1:27).

Now, let's bring this closer to home. While sources vary in their estimation of the exact number, over twenty thousand–plus children die every day across the globe of preventable diseases.[4] The lack of clean water, good nutrition, and proper medical treatment leads to this horrifying number. When I first came across this statistic, I couldn't stop thinking about it. I thought about how kids in our culture are often upset when they can't have an ice cream cone, brand-name shoes, or a cell phone. We definitely live in a First World bubble of privilege and excess. To break our own children out of this entitlement bubble for at least a short time, my husband has taken each one of our chidren separately on trips to Guatemala. There they have seen children so thankful for one bowl of rice a day—their only meal. Sometimes I want to live in my own little world and forget about kids who don't have enough to eat or who have worms in their feet because they have no shoes. Our Guatemalan missionary friend says that having worm-infested feet is normal to them. I want to cry every time I think about it.

We can't "fix it." Poverty is complex and widespread. So what does God want us to do? After reading Jeremiah's messages to the people, I know what God wants us *not* to do, and that's ignore it. We simply cannot continue to ignore poverty.

Although we can't solve the problem, each of us can play a role in helping others. There are so many great organizations that offer child-sponsorship opportunities, community feeding and housing programs, tutoring in low-income schools, and the list goes on. Though we are not called to them all, we are called to do *something*. Proverbs 21:13 says, "Those who shut their ears to the cries of the poor / will be ignored in their own time of need." We can't just shake our heads, cover our ears, and say "La, la, la. I don't hear the cries of the poor, Lord."

I encourage you to pray and ask God how you can get involved in answering the cries of the poor with your time, talents, and treasure. Look at your budget and consider what sacrifice you can make—great or small—to help a child in need live a full life. You won't regret it. Giving to those in need is always a win-win. Why, then, don't we do it as often and as generously as we should?

Jeremiah can help us with this question, but first I want to share the story of Vicky Talbot. In 2008, Vicky was diagnosed with a peptic ulcer, a possible ovarian cyst, and irritable bowel syndrome after many doctor visits and complaints of bloating and pain in her abdomen. Since Vicky was only twenty-five years old, the doctors didn't take her very seriously. They ran tests that showed no abnormalities and sent her home with antacid pills. By the time they realized she had bowel cancer, her tumor was the size of an orange.[5] The doctors offered Vicky superficial treatments for what could have been fatal. It was a case of misdiagnosis.

Just two chapters apart, Jeremiah repeats a similar story of misdiagnosis. God doesn't want us to miss this, so lean in close in your spirit as you read God's words through his prophet:

> "From the least to the greatest,
> their lives are ruled by greed.
> From prophets to priests,
> they are all frauds.

> They offer superficial treatments
> for my people's mortal wound.
> They give assurances of peace
> when there is no peace."
>
> (Jeremiah 6:13-14)

> "I will give their wives to others
> and their farms to strangers.
> From the least to the greatest,
> their lives are ruled by greed.
> Yes, even my prophets and priests are like that.
> They are all frauds.
> They offer superficial treatments
> for my people's mortal wound.
> They give assurances of peace
> when there is no peace."
>
> (Jeremiah 8:10-11)

In these two short passages God is saying a mouthful. He is outraged. This is one of those passages from Jeremiah that rings so true in our culture. Twice God said they were offering superficial treatments for His people's mortal wound.

"From the least to the greatest" their lives are ruled by what? Greed! It wasn't just the kings. It wasn't just the poor. Everyone was consumed with the need for stuff. Those who had a lot wanted more. Those who had little wanted more. We often don't see ourselves as greedy and neglecting the poor, but the truth is that when we are consumed with a desire for more—a nicer house, a better vacation, even simple things like new carpet—we can allow greed to rule our hearts. It's not about the things themselves; it's about the place they take in our hearts. God wants to give us good gifts but not to have those gifts take priority over Him.

Aren't greed and the desire for "more" what our world offers as well? They tell us through commercials, billboards, movies, and TV shows that things, people, and status will make us happy. The culture presents images of fame, romance, or some new product as the answer for the ache deep in our hearts. It is a superficial treatment for the mortal wound that is our need for a relationship with God. Whenever we settle for stuff to fulfill us, it's like putting a bandage over a bloody, gaping wound. It's a superficial treatment. Sin is the mortal wound that separates us from Him. We need Christ, not more stuff!

With that brief exploration of these verses, consider how you would feel if Vicky Talbot was your daughter or sister. Really feel it. Now consider that we're all God's daughters and sons, and He is hoppin' mad that we are taking antacids when cancer is growing in our souls. We need Him desperately. In fact, Christ is the only true healer of our hurt. We all have the God-shaped hole, and it's a mortal wound. Putting status, athletics, appearance, pills, possessions, or even other people in there will not fix it. So when the world offers these as remedies for our mortal wound, our Daddy gets upset.

God is understandably concerned about how we manage what He has entrusted to us. So here are a few questions we can ask ourselves:

- Am I offering God my firstfruits by tithing to my church?
- Am I praying for those who are truly in need—whether around the corner or around the world?
- Am I willing to go see with my own eyes and make the needs known to those around me?
- Will I cast a vision for those in my sphere of influence by

> my words and example, communicating that God has given us money not only to spend on ourselves but also to use for His kingdom?

Let's be intentional and evaluate our finances. We stop to get a coffee, pay a few bills, go to a movie, and then we wonder why we can't pay for car repairs when something breaks. Those of us who live in America are considered wealthy by the world's standards, yet most of us complain frequently about how expensive everything is and how we need more money—myself included. Everything we have has been provided to us by our Creator, including the skills or abilities that enable us to earn money. Realizing that our possessions are entrusted to us for our use instead of being entitlements helps us not be consumed with a desire for more and give more freely to those in need.

Sadly, our hearts are so prone to wander that sometimes we grow impatient, deciding that God's not fulfilling promises fast enough or giving us what we need when we need it. And like the people in Jeremiah's day, we take matters into our own hands.

Making a Fake

When God seems silent or distant, our inclination is often to "make a fake"—to meet our need by creating our own "god" or substitute. When I was a young mom with an infant, twin toddlers, and a kindergartner, I felt like I was drowning in duties. Diapers, discipline, and laundry caused me to look for relief. Thinking that the answer to my overload was my husband's helping more, I set up in my mind that if he would just do certain tasks, I would find peace and hope and joy. I made a fake by expecting my husband to be my savior rather than my spouse. He is a great helper at home, but I looked to him to alleviate my stress with unrealistic expectations. Anything can become a counterfeit god when we look to it as the solution to fix all our problems.

We know that the people of Judah had the same tendency because Jeremiah reveals to us their fascination with fakes. When the going got tough, instead of clinging to the God of their ancestors, they decided to make themselves some new gods. Oh, they weren't original gods; they borrowed them from many of the surrounding nations. Perhaps they had surmised that their God had lost His power or was weaker than the gods of Babylon, Egypt, and Assyria since those nations had become the playmakers with wealth, power, and control. Apparently, they had decided their religion was outdated and needed a modern makeover. So what if they tweaked it a little to make it better? That's harmless, right?

Actually, when it comes to the sovereign Creator and Ruler of the universe, we must dare to hope in Him and His way—not in our way by "making fakes." As we see in these verses from Jeremiah 10, God holds nothing back about the ridiculous notion of making our own gods:

> "Their gods are like
> helpless scarecrows in a cucumber field!
> They cannot speak,
> and they need to be carried because they
> cannot walk.
> Do not be afraid of such gods,
> for they can neither harm you nor do you
> any good...."

> People who worship idols are stupid and foolish.
> The things they worship are made of wood!
> They bring beaten sheets of silver from Tarshish
> and gold from Uphaz,
> and they give these materials to skillful craftsmen
> who make their idols.
> Then they dress these gods in royal blue and purple robes
> made by expert tailors.
> But the LORD is the only true God.
> He is the living God and the everlasting King!
> The whole earth trembles at his anger.
> The nations cannot stand up to his wrath.
>
> Say this to those who worship other gods: "Your so-called gods, who did not make the heavens and earth, will vanish from the earth and from under the heavens." (vv. 5, 8-11)

To put it simply, idols aren't real, and God is! That's really what it comes down to here. When we are disappointed with God because of our circumstances or His lack of intervention in our troubled lives, we are likely to come up with our own plan instead of following His. We're often tempted to manipulate and massage our situation instead of waiting for God.

As we turn back the pages of Scripture, we see others who tried to do this. Abraham's wife, Sarah, got tired of waiting for God to fulfill His promise of a son, so she attempted to "help" God out by giving her maidservant to sleep with her husband. If you're familiar with the story, you know how that turned out—not very well! Rebekah knew that God had said her younger son, Jacob, would be greater than the older twin, Esau. But rather than trusting in God's plan, she, too, tried to force the outcome God had already promised by leading Jacob to deceive his father. Suffice it to say that her plan didn't go exactly as planned. Our plans rarely do when we get ahead of God.

Did you notice what God compared the people's idols to in verse 5? Scarecrows. I can't read this verse without thinking of my East Texas grandpa. Listen for the accent in my paraphrase: "Those idols are about as lifeless as scarecrows in a melon patch." God was comparing their idols to lifeless straw figures that have no power—neither to help nor to harm. The fact that God mentions these scarecrows are in a melon patch—or cucumber patch, as some versions translate it—is interesting and significant.

Melons and cucumbers have something in common. They grow on the ground on a vine with leaves that camouflage them. For years I sent my kids out to gather the cucumbers from our garden. When they were little, they said there weren't any cucumbers ready to pick. So I took them out and showed them how to investigate and look a little harder for the cucumbers hidden among the leaves and vines. Scarecrows are lifeless, but they do scare birds away and keep them from eating crops such as berries or corn. Their value is worthless, however, in a cucumber or melon patch where the harvest is well hidden just the way God made it.

God goes to great lengths here in Jeremiah to convince us of the emptiness of our idolatry. He wants us to see Him in contrast to a useless scarecrow meant to guard crops that are already protected. While the scarecrow is lifeless and worthless, God is real and powerful. He is the Creator of life, and He is the only One able to protect us from real threats to our souls. Yet how often does our lack of faith keep us trusting in scarecrows instead of the true God who has our best interests at heart?

If I really believe God is who He says He is in His Word, then I won't worry so much about my children's health. I will pray more and manipulate less. I will see my own sin and blind spots and be less focused on the shortcomings of others. Sometimes my attitudes, actions, and lack of prayer reveal that I am making my own backups instead of trusting fully in God's ability to care for me. Often, I fashion a god that doesn't intervene, a god that's involved only in the "big" things instead of the details, a god who is waiting for me to mess up. But that is my personal counterfeit god—not the true and living God. It's a scarecrow in a cucumber patch.

Sometimes we can create a counterfeit god in our minds, thinking of God as how we perceive Him rather than looking to His Word for the truth about who He is. Have you ever found yourself doing that? Whenever we start to "make a fake," there's an amazing verse that can help to clear up any misconceptions we might have about what our God is like: "O Sovereign LORD! You made the heavens and earth by your strong hand and powerful arm. Nothing is too hard for you!" (Jeremiah 32:17).

Our God is no lifeless scarecrow! He made the earth with His strong hand and powerful arm, and *nothing* is too difficult for Him—not your relationship or family problems, your finances, or your work or church difficulties. Not even the most difficult person in your life!

Counterfeits are dangerous for all of us. Jeremiah warned God's people so they could recognize where they had been trading the real deal for a fake. He longed for his people to embrace the living God rather than chase empty idols. In the same way, we must remember God and evaluate our lives to see where we may be elevating people, positions, or possessions above Him in our hearts. We can dare to hope in the truth that we serve a loving God who longs to bring us back when we have strayed!

Dare to Hope Challenge

One of the best ways to guard against a counterfeit is to learn to spot a fake, and the way we learn to spot a fake is by studying the original—the genuine article. Experts spend many hours studying a genuine bill in order to identify counterfeit dollars; likewise, we can spot counterfeit gods by studying the truth of who God is. Be intentional in studying the character of the one true God. Begin by listing as many character traits of God as you can think of—traits such as almighty, caring, faithful, gracious, holy, infinite, just, loving, majestic, never changing, omnipresent, omniscient, self-sufficient, wise. (If you want, think of one word for each letter of the alphabet.) Over a period of time, look up each word in a Bible concordance and read some of the passages listed for that word. Praise God for these wonderful attributes, acknowledging that idols could never compare to our awe-inspiring God!

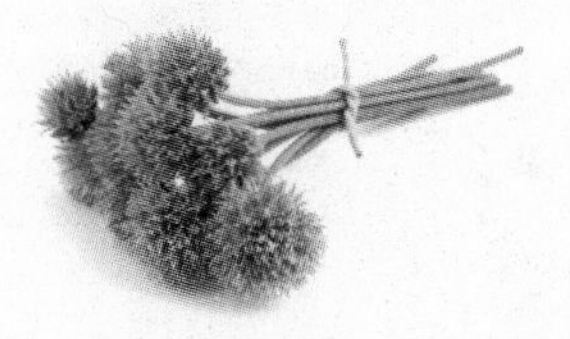

CHAPTER 3

Opening Our Ears

Listen

Ask me and I will tell you remarkable secrets you do not know about things to come.

—Jeremiah 33:3

I love sixth-grade girls. They are eager, silly, and never at a loss for words. For many years I led a small group of sixth-grade girls, and we often talked about issues going on in their middle-school lives, such as problems with friends, teachers, and, of course, boys. One day one of the girls was telling a story in great detail about a misunderstanding with her teacher. I asked what her mom thought about the situation, because if she had all the facts straight, this parent would be one upset momma. I was shocked to find that this girl had not discussed what was going on with either her mom or dad.

I was intrigued. Of the five girls in the room, all agreed that they don't tell their parents most of what is really going on in their hearts and minds. Panic rose inside me because at the time I had twin fifth-grade girls. *Will they stop talking to me next year?* I wondered. I pressed further. Did they think their parents would punish them? Would they overreact? Why the lack of communication?

In a small group, these girls were never a quiet bunch. However, the resounding response was something like this: "My parents don't listen; when I talk, I can see they are thinking about something else. They are busy and preoccupied, and my little school or friend problems aren't important to them. Eventually, I just quit telling them all the details because they don't listen anyway or they act like the things I'm concerned about are silly or unimportant." This composite of multiple responses alarmed me.

When I went home after leaving my sweet sixth-grade girls and sat down with my daughters to inquire about my own listening skills, I wasn't prepared for their responses. They had some similar feelings. "You're always on the computer or phone or working in the kitchen, and you seem distracted or even irritated when I try to tell you something." Though I had to admit that I had a lot on my mind most of the time, I didn't want my girls to stop talking to me and find other ears willing to listen. Later when they would have questions about their friends, boys, and even their faith, I didn't want to discover I'd lost the opportunity because I didn't take the time to listen when they had a long, detailed story about the characters in a book they were reading or the ongoing saga of how Emily and Jennifer weren't getting along at school.

I began to wonder: *if my listening skills aren't the greatest with my own children, who are physically present and asking for my attention, how much easier is it for me to struggle with listening to my Creator God?* This is a question we all need to ask. Are we really listening?

In the Book of Jeremiah there is a theme that is repeated again and again, and this repetition tells us that God wants to be sure we don't miss it either: God wants His people to open their ears and listen to Him. Throughout the book we see that God calls His people to listen, and no one is exempt from this call to hear God.

The Hebrew word translated into English as "hearken," "hear," or "listen" is *shama*, which means "to hear with attention or interest."[1] *Shama*, which occurs over one thousand times in the Old Testament, is a familiar word to many of us, because it refers to what became a very important element of Judaism following the exile. It also was familiar to the people of Judah during Jeremiah's time because the cornerstone of their monotheistic faith in one God, which set them apart from the polytheistic nations surrounding them, is found in Deuteronomy 6:4, known as the Shema or Shama: "Listen, O Israel! The LORD is our God, the LORD alone." One source explains that "the Shema is the central prayer in the Jewish prayerbook (Siddur) and is often the first section of Scripture that a Jewish child learns. During its recitation in the synagogue, Orthodox Jews pronounce each word very carefully and cover their eyes with their right hand. Many Jews recite the Shema at least twice daily: once in the morning and once in the evening."[2]

In Jeremiah's time, the people failed to listen, and God got their attention by allowing them to be taken captive. It is interesting that during the time of Ezra when the people returned after seventy years of captivity, just as Jeremiah had prophesied, the Jewish book of prayer (Siddur) first surfaced. Perhaps the Shema became the central prayer because the people realized the consequences of their closed ears and wanted to be careful not to repeat their mistakes.

The opposite of closed ears is open ears. So what does it mean to have ears that are open to God? It means to listen, respond, cooperate, maintain focus, and prove with your actions that you have heard what God is saying. Would those closest to you describe you as quick to listen, responsive, cooperative, focused, and consistently living a life that reflects the faith you claim? If we're honest, we must admit that we, too, struggle with closed spiritual ears. Despite the gifts of God's living Word, His Spirit, His body of believers (the church), and the life of His beloved Son, we often find ourselves distracted and stubborn like the peers of Jeremiah. In our digital age of quick information, I find my mind wandering when trying to read for long periods of time. I also notice that in my prayer life I often do a lot of talking and struggle to take time to be still and listen. More than ever, we need intentionality in spiritual disciplines so that we don't miss hearing God's still small voice in a fast-paced world.

Two short passages in the New Testament say so succinctly what Jeremiah tried in desperation to communicate, showing us that the concept of spiritual ears has not changed with the new covenant; Shama is still God's desire for us:

> Then he added, "Pay close attention to what you hear. The closer you listen, the more understanding you will be given—and you will receive even more. To those who listen to my teaching, more understanding will be given. But for those who are not listening, even what little understanding they have will be taken away from them." (Mark 4:24-25)

> Be careful that you do not refuse to listen to the One who is speaking. For if the people of Israel did not escape when they refused to listen to Moses, the earthly messenger, we will certainly not escape if we reject the One who speaks to us from heaven! When God spoke from Mount Sinai his voice shook the earth, but now he makes another promise: "Once again I will shake not only the earth but the heavens also." This means that all of creation will be shaken and removed, so that only unshakable things will remain. (Hebrews 12:25-27)

We may not have a prophet proclaiming God's message to us in the street, but God is still calling us to listen to His message. I pray that we will not be so distracted by the minutia of daily life that we fail to hear. So let me ask you: How are your listening skills? How open are you to what God is saying to you? I've learned from personal experience that if we think He isn't speaking, then chances are we haven't been taking sufficient time to listen well.

The inside of our heads can be a very noisy place. I have found that spending time in quiet teaches me to listen to God. When I am silent and focused on God, I begin to notice what He is saying to me through His creation, the people around me, His Holy Spirit, my circumstances, and His word. Being quiet and curious opens my ears to hear from God. Let's explore together how we can do this in our everyday lives.

Reading with Curiosity

Curious George is one of my favorite children's book series. The man with the yellow hat is always patient with George even though he gets into so much trouble because of his curiosity. George's caregiver knows the curious monkey isn't willfully rebelling; he just wants to know and discover things about the world. While Curious George could have a few more boundaries, we could learn from him how to be more curious.

When my adorable niece Sophia was younger, I would read her Curious George books, and one day it hit me that although George's curiosity gets him in trouble, it also is the thing that usually solves the larger problem at hand. In one particular story about a puppy that gets lost, George accidentally opens all the cages at a kennel. Although his curiosity initially causes chaos, the lost puppy is

The clay doesn't get to choose
what kind of vessel it turns out to be;
it has to trust the potter's
best judgment.

found through the process of rounding up the puppies, and George becomes a hero.

I believe God wants us to use the brain He has given us to question, discuss, and work through the things we don't understand. Sometimes this creates some initial chaos, but it ends up helping us work through bigger issues of faith and relationships.

This includes how we approach Scripture. The Prophets especially can be books we steer away from, thinking they are too difficult to understand or not relevant to our lives. Yet I believe God has a timeless message for us in the pages of Jeremiah.

I have found in my own life that if I approach God's Word with curiosity—with a few simple questions in mind—I am usually overwhelmed by what God has to teach me. These are the questions I ask myself as I read:

- What will I learn about God—who He is, how He interacts with people, what the verses say about His character?
- What will I learn about myself—how I approach or do not approach Him, what He calls me to do or not to do, how He expresses His love to me, what keeps me from experiencing Him more fully?
- Is there anything that God is specifically saying about my current thoughts, attitudes, or actions?

When we read passages such as Jeremiah 18:1-12 with curiosity, we learn so much about God's character and our need for God:

> The LORD gave another message to Jeremiah. He said, "Go down to the potter's shop, and I will speak to you there." So I did as he told me and found the

> potter working at his wheel. But the jar he was making did not turn out as he had hoped, so he crushed it into a lump of clay again and started over.
>
> Then the LORD gave me this message: "O Israel, can I not do to you as this potter has done to his clay? As the clay is in the potter's hand, so are you in my hand.

The clay doesn't get to choose what kind of vessel it turns out to be; it has to trust the potter's best judgment. This is difficult for me. I want God to work things out in a way that makes sense to me. I want to pick the color, use, and shape of how I will turn out. And I certainly don't want to be fired in a kiln! However, God gives us this illustration of who He is to help us understand what we often forget: He is the Potter; we are the clay.

The Hebrew word used for the potter in these verses is *yatsar*, which means "to form, fashion, frame."[3] This is the same word used in Genesis 2:7-8 for God's creation of man from clay. Then in Jeremiah 1:5, this same word is used to describe how God formed Jeremiah in the womb. God is telling us that He is the former, fashioner, and framer in our lives. Just as the people of Judah needed to surrender to God's instrument, Babylon, we need to surrender to the Potter, trusting that if He allows us to go through the fire, it will be to strengthen us for use in His kingdom.

As the Potter, God sovereignly chooses what gifts and talents to give us, what family to place us in, and how to develop our endurance. Yet we are the ones who control the consistency of our clay. Will we be stiff and resistant like the stubborn people of Judah with closed ears, or will we be soft and moldable, willing to endure pressure, trimming, and fire in order to become vessels for His use? The choice is ours to make.

When we read the Book of Jeremiah with curiosity, we not only see God as the Potter but we also learn about His mighty power. One name that is used for God more than eighty times throughout the book—and over two hundred times throughout Scripture—is "Lord Sabaoth." Depending on the version, this name for God is translated "the Lord of Heaven's Armies, the Lord Almighty, the Lord of Hosts, or the Lord of Armies."[4] The Hebrew word *Sabaoth* is a military term in the Hebrew meaning "to wage war." In this name for God we remember that He commands the armies of heaven and has authority over the celestial bodies (Isaiah 40:26; Genesis 2:1), the angels (Psalm 103:20-21), the armies of Israel (Exodus 12:41), and all who trust in Him (Psalm 46:7, 11).[5]

These insights help us to see that "Lord Sabaoth" is used to remind us of who our God really is: the powerful Commander in Chief with all of the angels at His disposal. Our problems are never too big for Him. He is holy, sovereign, and able to do what He says He will do; and if we will listen and really get to know Him as we study His Word with curiosity, we will find that He is more than worthy of our complete trust and confidence.

How does it feel to know that you have access to the Commander in Chief of the whole world—the whole *universe*? I love how Jeremiah shows us the strong side of God's power as Lord Sabaoth while also showing God as the artist sitting at the potter's wheel, carefully shaping us into His image. Our God is both powerful and personal, and He wants each of us to know Him better. In fact, He wants *you* to ask Him questions and wait in His presence for answers.

I often laugh with God at how amazingly precise He is at speaking to my struggles or answering a specific question—such as when I asked Him why Jeremiah isn't written in chronological order but seems to skip all over the place. You see, I am a "go in order" kind of girl, and so I noticed immediately that the themes in Jeremiah are not neat and orderly but scattered throughout the book. Minutes after asking God about this, I read Ecclesiastes 7:13 in my daily quiet time: "Accept the way God does things, / for who can straighten what he has made crooked?" God directly answered my question! This has happened to me so many times that it no longer surprises me. In fact, I have come to anticipate it.

I expect God to get my attention because I am committed to closeness with Him. At this point, I watch for details in Scripture to jump out at me. When we create a life of closeness with God through daily Scripture reading and prayer, we begin to see patterns of grace, hope, and understanding. But we have to stay close, *really close*!

Clinging Like Underwear

Do you like loose, baggy underwear? Most of us don't—though some guys wear boxers, which aren't as snug as briefs. But all of us could say that we want our underwear to fit, right? Why this talk of underwear? Believe me, this girl who was raised in Texas does not enjoy public conversations of private things. It doesn't take much to make me blush. However, God is the one who mentions the "unmentionables"!

In Jeremiah 13 we discover that God wants us to cling to Him like a loincloth to a waist; and in those days, a loincloth was essentially *underwear*. Yes, you read that right! God wants us to cling to Him like underwear.

God told the prophet Jeremiah to buy a loincloth, wear it for a while, and then hide it in a crevice in the rocks. Then later, when God told Jeremiah to go back and get it, he found that it was ruined and useless. God used a very practical object lesson to illustrate what happens when we do not cling to Him. There are three practical insights we can draw from this illustration.

First, God wants a *close* relationship with us. We often talk *about* God, fitting Him in where it is culturally acceptable. But how close is your relationship with Him? Do you tell Him exciting news? When the world is falling apart around you, is He the one you run to for help and support? Do your calendar and bank account reveal that He is your closest friend?

God is holy and sovereign—the Potter who molds us the way He chooses and the Lord of Heaven's Armies, as we've seen. Yet God chooses to speak to us in ways that we can understand, including using underwear as an analogy; and God has said that He wants us to cling to Him like underwear.

Underwear is not only supposed to be close, it is also *personal.* Undergarments are personal. We don't show them to everyone. So a second insight is that God wants our relationship with Him to be personal.

There is one more important thing about underwear. It is meant to be worn *daily*. When my girls were younger and I would fold laundry, sometimes I would notice that one of my daughter's panty piles was lower than the others; so I would give her a reminder—you know, to change it every day! Likewise, God wants us to be in constant, daily contact with Him.

God wants us to know Him—and not just through ritualistic religious function. That's what was happening in Judah, and it caused their intimacy with God to be reduced to rot because they tucked closeness with Him into a dark hole. God used Jeremiah to illustrate this point with a loincloth worn close to the body. And I love that it was an illustration *everyone* could relate to—because priests as well as common people wore loincloths. God wants all people to cling to Him by entering into a close relationship with Him. The Hebrew word for "cling" (*dabaq*) used in Jeremiah 13:11 is the same word used in Genesis 2:24: "a man leaves his father and mother and clings to his wife" (NRSV). It means "to cling, stick, stay close, cleave, keep close, stick to, stick with, follow closely, join to, over-take, catch."[6] The result of clinging like that is intimacy.

So what kept the people from enjoying this intimacy with God? It boils down to pride. They shifted their focus from God and His Word to more tangible things they could taste and touch. For them, these tangible things were idols. As they worshipped the Queen of Heaven and made idols out of wood, they slowly drifted away from the true God. Instead of staying in close relationship with God and His Word, they chose to do what they wanted. And that's when pride crept in. Of course, this didn't happen overnight. They didn't wake up one day and decide not to worship the true God. Instead, one small choice after another caused a domino effect until they found themselves moving in a totally different direction.

The people quit listening to God even though they had prophets like Jeremiah; even though they had portions of God's Word; even though they had oral storytelling about what God had done through Noah, Abraham, Moses, and King David. Today we have an even fuller revelation of God—His complete Word. Not only that, we also have access to some of the best Bible teaching available twenty-four hours a day through the internet, podcasts, Christian TV and radio, and more books and commentaries than we could read in a lifetime—all to help us know, love, and understand who God is and what He wants to do in our lives. But the heart of the matter is this: Are we listening to the voice of God, or are we listening to the voices of our culture? Remember, He wants us to cling to Him like underwear, to stay close.

Our problem is that we are forgetful, forgetting God like that forgotten loincloth among the rocks. I can be on a mountaintop worshipping God at an event and a week later feel a million miles away from Him, consumed with my to-do list. Just as we change our underwear every day, we need to renew our closeness with God every day. We need to open our ears and listen.

Our copy of God's Word shouldn't be something we search *for* to take to church on Sundays; it should be something we search *in* daily so that we can hear from Him. When we read God's Word expectantly, we want to know who He is, how He wants us to live, and what things He challenges us to be cautious about. We shouldn't just talk *about* God; we should talk *with* God about everything we are thinking and feeling. The question is, do we?

It blows my mind that the Lord of Heaven's Armies really can use even the underwear we put on every day to call us back to Him. He is all-knowing, all-powerful, and the Creator of everything I see. Yet if I'm honest, sometimes I would rather spend time watching TV, chatting on the phone with my sisters and friends, and surfing on social media than connecting with the God of the universe. When I say I've been so busy I haven't had time to read my Bible and pray, I know it's a lie. We all make time for what we really want to do. I know I do. In my pride, often I'd rather do what feels good in the moment than make choices that will lead to intimacy with Christ. But whenever we do choose to come before Him and listen, we are blessed beyond measure. His love and truth wash over us as He counsels, encourages, and reminds us about His great love for us. His loving voice speaks truth to us even when life gets noisy.

Listening to the Right Voices

Every day we are bombarded by different voices. My mailbox overflows with mail from companies trying to sell me something. Catalogs, advertisements of everything from oil changes to carpet cleaning, and credit card offers abound. Then I can browse through social media or turn on the news and see others advocating strong political causes they want us to jump on the bandwagon to support. In the checkout line, messages call me to be skinny and fit so that I will feel good about myself. There's no shortage of voices in the Christian realm either. I once saw some video clips online from a discussion between major church leaders. The dialogue mostly consisted of pastors discussing how the modern church should approach preaching, evangelism, and discipleship.

It's great to talk, debate, and work through the issues related to trying to follow God. I'm not saying the voices are all bad. I need the news and my social media friends to keep me up-to-date on things going on in the government of which I otherwise might not be aware. But how can we know that we are following the right leaders, listening to the right voices, and walking in God's truth in the many arenas of life?

We don't want to be like the people of Judah in Jeremiah's day who didn't listen to God but chose to listen to "others" with a more popular message like the religious priests and prophets. They called for tolerance, freedom of expression (idolatry), and permissiveness. Sound familiar? Is it possible that we are listening to the "others" of our day instead of God's true messengers? How can we know for sure?

Let's consider three insights God has for us in Jeremiah 23 related to discerning which voices we should heed.

1. Consider the moral character of the messenger.

First, as we seek to understand how to discern the validity of a message, we must take a look at the personal integrity of the mouthpiece. Although we must be careful about judging our leaders or expecting perfection from them, we should consider if their lives reflect their own teaching. In other words, does their walk match their talk?

God's heart breaks over these people who claim to speak for God but make up their own messages.

In Jeremiah 23:9-17, God speaks through Jeremiah that even the priests and prophets were committing ungodly acts right in the temple of God. He mentions their adultery and dishonesty. The indictment also mentions that they encouraged others in doing evil and failed to warn the people of their sins. Verse 17 reads,

> "They keep saying to those who despise my word,
> 'Don't worry! The LORD says you will
> have peace!'
> And to those who stubbornly follow their own desires,
> they say, 'No harm will come your way!' "

So we must evaluate the messenger's life as we consider the validity of their message.

When we are listening to the voices of politicians, preachers, or individuals on TV, we need to exercise discernment as we look at their lives and see if their behaviors are in line with what we know about God and His character. As one source points out, "The prophet always stood for God's standards and called people to Him..., and it was this that distinguished a true prophet from a false prophet."[7]

Jesus confirmed Jeremiah's call to evaluate the life of the messenger when he warned us about false prophets in Matthew 7, saying that false prophets are disguised as harmless sheep while beneath that veneer they are vicious wolves. He called us to look not only at what others say but also at how they act. Our judgments about others shouldn't lead us to gossip, shaming, or self-righteousness but should cause us to make sure that those who teach us God's Word are walking in a way that matches their talk.

Of course, everyone sins, so no one will perfectly live out God's standards; but we should not see blatant discord between a teacher's life and message. As Jesus said, a tree is "identified by its fruit" (Luke 6:44). Just as Jeremiah compared the fruit tree planted by the river to the dry, stunted shrub in the desert, Jesus said we are to listen to those whose lives are characterized by good fruit.

2. Evaluate the message to see if it lines up with God's Word.

As we saw in the last chapter, just as experts spend time studying a genuine bill in order to identify counterfeit dollars, so we must continually study the truth of God's Word in order to recognize error. This will prepare us to exercise discernment when the many voices in our life and culture present us with information. Jeremiah used a helpful analogy when he said,

> "Let these false prophets tell their dreams,
> but let my true messengers faithfully
> proclaim my every word.
> There is a difference between straw and grain!"
> (Jeremiah 23:28)

One commentator helps us understand his words this way: "Dreams of the false prophets were to the word of God as chaff to wheat. Words of false prophets have no value; those of the true messengers of God are as wheat, as food for believers."[8] Straw and grain may share some common physical characteristics, but their function couldn't be more dissimilar. While straw was collected for bedding, grain was useful for nourishment. The message of the false prophets had no lasting value. It provided temporary comfort like the straw used to make beds for people and animals in that day, but it wasn't of any value to feed them.

God's Word is alive and active. It may deal out severe truth at times, but wouldn't we rather hear painful truth than comforting lies? I mean, who wants to be deceived? So when we find "straw" creeping into our spiritual diets, we need to remember Jeremiah's message in order to keep from being tempted to numb our problems with soul "junk food"—such as escaping into a novel, playing online games, or zoning out in front of the TV. These things aren't inherently bad, but they are not the spiritual food God says we need in order to grow. God wants to immerse us in His truth, but we often settle for a popular, comforting message instead.

Take a moment for a personal inventory. Is there a nagging in your spirit about any of the voices you are allowing to speak into your soul? Things like TV, books, music, games, social media, magazines, newspapers, friends, pastors, teachers, talk radio, even Bible studies? The point is that we are called to evaluate the many modes of information flooding our brains on any given day, because an overload can desensitize us to hidden messages that do not line up with God's Word. So would you say you're eating grain, or are you lying in a bed of straw, feeling empty even after eating your fill? The latter can make you cranky—believe me, I know from experience!

Speaking of lying in straw, it can also make you itchy. Paul wrote that a time was coming when people would want to hear comforting lies with itching ears (2 Timothy 4:3-4). I believe this describes our culture. We are creatures of comfort, yet God cares more about our character than our comfort.

I remember a time when I was begging God to take away a situation in my life that was about as comfortable as wearing three-inch heels while running a marathon. Some personal misunderstandings between friends put me in the middle of a complicated predicament. I had to measure every word, test my heart motives, and beg God for wisdom as I approached both sides. I wasn't always sure when to stay out of their disagreement and when God was calling me to engage in the fracture. When we avoided the subject, it felt like an elephant in the room no one was acknowledging; but I found that addressing it sometimes added fuel to the fire of conflict. As much as I hated to admit it at the time, though, I knew that this difficult situation was the very thing conforming me to God's image and growing my faith.

Sometimes eating grain requires discipline and perseverance. It may be painful going down, but it brings amazing growth. If God's Word is to be our measuring rod for evaluating the messages we receive, then it is important for us to consider how well we know God's Word.

The people Jeremiah spoke to didn't know God's Word, so they weren't able to discern when others twisted it. He said that they did not know the Lord's laws (Jeremiah 8:7-9). The challenge for many believers today is not only to know God's standards but also to take time to sift through the way others are applying those truths in today's culture. I know it can be daunting. After all, there are sixty-six books written by more than forty authors over a period of fourteen hundred years. And, of course, the original languages of the Bible were not English. Yet the fact that there are different theological positions and interpretations within the body of Christ compels us to know and understand what we believe and why. Taking the time to read, study, question, and discern the truth can seem overwhelming in the midst of doctors' appointments, soccer practice, homework, and work schedules, but here's a question we must ask ourselves: *When I get to the end of my life and stand before my heavenly Father, what will have seemed so important that I didn't have time to read and study the living book He gave us?*

Ouch, right? When I consider the hours I've spent watching TV, chattering about nothing on the phone, or reading social media posts, I know the issue is not one of not having enough time. It's about how I choose to spend my time. We all have time wasters we can weed out of our lives; and if we're going to cut something out, we can be ready to fill that space with God's Word before a new time waster claims its spot!

We may not have prophets shouting messages from the street corners, but we do have ready access to the complete revelation of God's Word—often in a variety of versions and formats; not to mention easy access to godly men and women teaching God's Word and making their messages available through a variety of media. Give some thought to times in your day when you might take advantage of reading or listening to God's Word—such as when exercising, driving in the car, doing chores, and winding down at the end of the day. A little creativity and intentionality can help us to know God's Word so that we can evaluate the many messages of our culture.

3. Ask the right questions.

We question everything today, from where to find the best deal to the decisions made at the PTO meeting. But when it comes to God's Word, we sometimes just recite rote prayers or fly through a passage so we can check Bible reading off our to-do list. God wants us to read His Word carefully, asking the right questions.

So much has been entrusted to us. Think about it: we have more truth than Moses and the prophets had. We have the Gospels, the letters of Paul, and more—the complete revelation of God. So we need to be careful to read and listen well to God's Word. Rather than just having "quiet time," we must ask the Holy Spirit to give us spiritual wisdom so that we may understand and apply the truths of Scripture in daily life. However we read or study God's Word, our approach should be active listening rather than passive acceptance, asking questions such as these:

What is being presented?
Does it line up with the whole of Scripture?
What is the historical and cultural context?
What interpretations do biblical scholars/commentaries offer?
What does it tell me about God's heart and character?
Where does this message need specific or general application in my life?

Asking the right questions is an important part of discerning truth. Our heart cry should be that of the psalmist: "O LORD, listen to my cry; / give me the discerning mind you promised" (Psalm 119:169). That's a prayer we can pray with confidence because God delights in our questions.

Keep Asking and Listening

My children never had a problem with asking. One day a few years ago my daughter asked if she could have a freezer pop. "How many have you had today?" I countered. "Just two," was her hopeful reply. They have no lack of restraint in asking. I remember one day when we were on our way home from a wonderful day at the zoo, and as we passed a water park the kids asked, "When can we go there?" It seems to be a universal phenomenon; children aren't afraid of asking.

As parents we're often trying to teach our children to ask for things less often, or at least to ask for more appropriate things. But God welcomes our asking. Why? Because asking means dialogue.

In and of itself, questioning is a good thing—within reason and when done with respect. We should never stuff our doubts. Doubts are real and everyone has them. What is most important is what we do with them. When we doubt, it should lead us to think, study, and ask questions.

I write specific questions I have for God all the time. I note them in my Bible next to a passage I don't understand and in my journal as I pray—everything from, "Are you calling me to go serve my sister-in-law, or is that just my idea?" to "How do you want me to prioritize my to-do list today?"

Jeremiah asked God questions too. They talked together regularly.

Our Father God wants us to ask, but we must learn to listen for His answers and trust that He is working for our good even when He doesn't give us what we request.

I remember a kind Sunday school teacher telling me when I was a child that God's phone number was 3-3-3. She was referring to Jeremiah 33:3: "Ask me and I will tell you remarkable secrets you do not know about things to come."

Jeremiah approached God with confidence, rehearsing characteristics about who God is and how He behaves. He asked specific questions. He expressed his frustrations over things that didn't make sense to him. He admitted his own faults and asked God to correct him when he was wrong. He dialogued with God.

There are many ways to pray, but when I was in junior high I was taught a simple way to pray that has stuck with me all these years. You may be familiar with this prayer method:

A doration
C onfession
T hanksgiving
S upplication (to request humbly)

We see these same elements in the prayers of others in the Bible who enjoyed intimacy with God. The prayers of Daniel, King David, and Hezekiah also reflect adoring or praising God for who He is, sometimes using a specific name such as the Lord of Heaven's Armies. There are many examples in the Bible of confessing or admitting that we need correcting, because we all make mistakes. Sometimes this is individual confession and sometimes it is corporate confession. Jeremiah confesses the sin of the whole nation before God. The Bible also reveals prayers of thankfulness, such as Mary's song when she finds out she is carrying the Messiah. We also find plenty of examples of asking God to intervene and save, such as David's psalms written when he was on the run from King Saul.

Of course, ACTS is not the only way to pray, since prayer is simply talking to God. However, a system such as this can be helpful to us. At first my children's prayers often sounded like this: "God, thanks for the wonderful day today, and I hope we have a wonderful day tomorrow." But after teaching them ACTS, they learned to connect with God on a deeper level.

However we choose to pray, we are engaging in dialogue with God. We see the consistency of asking, listening, and knowing God in prayer all the way from Jeremiah through the entire span of the New Testament. The theme is consistent: ask, ask, and ask; listen, listen, and listen some more! Regardless of how I pray, I've found that God mostly answers my questions through His Word—though sometimes He uses other books, people, and circumstances. One time I honestly got an answer through a name written on the license plate of the car in front of me while I was questioning God at a stoplight. It sounds crazy, I know, but I wholeheartedly believe it was a very direct and specific answer to my question. When God seems silent in my life, I usually find it's because I've either stopped asking questions or stopped taking the time to listen for the answers. What about you?

What is keeping you from an "underwear-close" relationship with God in your prayer life? Luke 11:8 in the New Living Translation talks about asking with "shameless persistence." We need to keep asking with the persistence of children when they want a treat or a favor. At the same time we must examine our motives. *Why* do we want what we're asking for? Is it for our own pleasure? Will it truly benefit us in the long run?

The bottom line is that our Father God wants us to ask, but we must learn to listen for His answers and trust that He is working for our good even when He doesn't give us what we request. As we read with curiosity, cling to Him like underwear, listen to the right voices, and keep on asking, we will find ourselves learning to hear His voice and trust that His answers are best!

Dare to Hope Challenge

Memorize Jeremiah 33:3:

> "Ask me and I will tell you remarkable secrets you do not know about things to come."

Each day as you put on your underwear, recite this verse and say a short prayer, inviting God to speak to you throughout the day. If this sounds like a silly practice to you, just remember that the metaphor of underwear was God's idea!

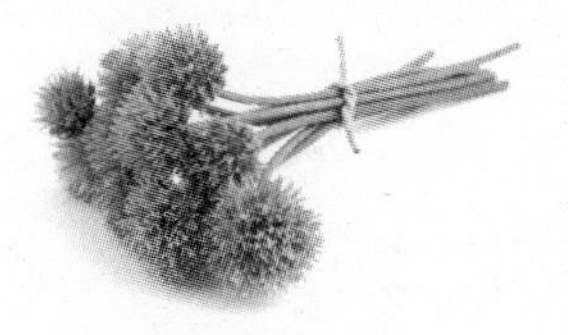

CHAPTER 4

Staying Spiritually Sensitive

Check Your Heart

"The human heart is the most deceitful of all things,
and desperately wicked.
Who really knows how bad it is?
But I, the Lord, search all hearts
and examine secret motives.
I give all people their due rewards,
according to what their actions deserve."
—Jeremiah 17:9-10

Staying spiritually sensitive is a heart issue, and heart issues can be complicated. At times we struggle to understand just what is going on inside of us. I remember a time when God revealed some hard-heartedness I didn't even know was there. It was painful. My heart literally hurt. My feelings could turn on a dime. One minute I was puffed up with self-righteousness, blaming others and feeling indignant about wrongs done to me, and the next I was broken and crying, wondering where I had erred in the latest blowup with a complicated relationship.

What I did know at the time, though, is that God was shattering some hardness in my heart. I knew I had some steps to take in making up with this person whose harsh words had hurt me. I also knew that my response was less than gracious. We seemed to misunderstand each other often. I knew that Christ calls me to be kind, loving, and forgiving as He is toward me. But I strugged to get my heart in line with God's truth when my feelings pulled me in another direction. This led me to bring my heart before my God and ask Him to help me sort through pain and perceptions so that He could restore softness in my most vital organ. I didn't want to stay hard-hearted, repeating the mistakes made by the people in Jeremiah's day.

Your heart may be full of joy, contentment, and peace today; and if so, God calls you to celebrate. Or perhaps you can relate to the hurt I've just described because you're struggling with a heart issue of your own. Perhaps your marriage is ending, your children are struggling, or someone you love is dying. No matter what our heart issues are right now, we must be careful to allow God full access to our hearts. This requires a willingness to deal with heart issues, because glossing over them, skipping to the next thing, and moving on in life without dealing with our hearts is much simpler than going through the softening process.

Many of us have skipped over heart issues for years—especially in relationships with family and friends. We stuff our pain and continue living our lives without dealing with it, giving resentment a chance to grow. But this allows our hearts to get hard, and a painful shattering process is often necessary to restore them. The great news, however, is that when we allow God to do the deep work in our hearts, it fosters closeness with Him in the midst of our brokenness that is unbelievably worth it!

So how do we get started? How can we allow God to restore the softness in our hearts?

Evaluating the Condition of Our Hearts

A helpful first step in the process of allowing God to soften our hearts is evaluating the condition of our hearts. Just as we go to the doctor when we're having symptoms that suggest we might have heart trouble, so we can prayerfully invite God to help us examine the spiritual condition of our hearts.

When we look at Jeremiah's proclamations from God to the people of Israel, we find some helpful truths and cautions about the condition of our hearts. First, Jeremiah tells us to be careful not to say that we haven't done anything wrong, that surely God couldn't be angry at us (Jeremiah 2:35). This requires self-awareness that comes from self-evaluation. We can ask God to reveal any blind spots. Then Jeremiah warns us not to make our faces like stone and refuse to repent (5:3). We must take a correctable posture. One practical idea is to pray the prayer of the psalmist in Psalm 141:5a:

> "Let the godly strike me!
> It will be a kindness!
> If they correct me, it is soothing medicine.
> Don't let me refuse it."

Jeremiah also tells us to ask God what wrongs we have done and avoid racing into sin like a horse galloping into battle (Jeremiah 8:6). We must be intentional with our thoughts, words, and actions so that we don't fall in with the herd of our culture that is running after sin. Finally, Jeremiah tells us to remember the sins of our ancestors, show remorse, repent, and follow God's Word (44:9-10). These are some steps we can take toward keeping a soft heart.

It all boils down to one simple truth: *we need to be more careful about what we do and do not do with our hearts.*

Without intentional evaluation, our hearts may become hard and insensitive—even apart from our awareness; then suddenly one day we wake up and find ourselves much like the people of Judah, claiming we're free of sin and refusing to say we're sorry. None of us wants to end up in that condition! Instead we want to learn from the people of Judah and make different choices to recognize and turn from our sin and allow God to soften our hearts.

This is the very reason the Israelites were disciplined by the Lord, because they refused to accept responsibility for their sin or ask for forgiveness. Jeremiah 17:1 relates these actions to the condition of their hearts:

> "The sin of Judah
> is inscribed with an iron chisel—
> engraved with a diamond point on their stony hearts
> and on the corners of their altars."

God found their hearts to be as hard as stone tablets, but it didn't happen overnight. Just as stones are formed over time—becoming hard, rough, and heavy—so the people's hearts gradually hardened as they made secret choices to self-protect, blame others for their problems, and refuse to acknowledge their own errors.

I wish I couldn't relate, but in my own relationships there are times when I build a wall of stone around my heart because I feel I've been wronged. As a pastor's wife, sometimes it's easier not to let people get too close. When you're in ministry and your friends are part of your church family, there are lonely times when you can't share your burdens with those friends in order to keep confidentiality and to guard against gossip. The more you risk in relationships, the more you have to lose. When you get burned a few times, it can be discouraging to keep putting yourself out there. And you certainly don't have to be in ministry to get burned! Each of us knows what it's like to be hurt by someone, and we can begin building a wall—waiting for the other person to apologize or change.

Here's what I've learned to be true. We can't change the hearts of others, but we can learn to put down our microscopes and pick up our own heart mirrors.

We can't change the hearts of others,
but we can learn to put down
our microscopes and pick up
our own heart mirrors.

Look at these harsh words Jeremiah wrote about the human heart:

> "The human heart is the most deceitful of all things,
> and desperately wicked.
> Who really knows how bad it is?"
>
> Jeremiah 17:9

These words of Jeremiah find confirmation in Proverbs 20:9: "Who can say, 'I have cleansed my heart; / I am pure and free from sin'?" Similarly, 1 John 1:10 tells us, "If we claim we have not sinned, we are calling God a liar and showing that his word has no place in our hearts." It seems there is always something for God to work on in our hearts! The truth is that we are never completely blameless in any conflict. Again, we can't fix others, but we *can* evaluate our own hearts and repent.

When it comes to evaluating our hearts, a helpful first step is asking questions such as these:

- Lord, why do I feel so sad, distracted, or empty?
- Why did that person's words or actions cut me so deeply?
- Why do I want to stay mad at that person?
- What part of my heart has grown hard, and what will it take to soften it again?

Other questions may come to mind as we evaluate our heart response in a particular situation. Asking questions and taking the time to understand our feelings begin the process of allowing God to do His transforming work in our hearts. But if we refuse to acknowledge the hurt or the hate, we can't move on to the healing.

Think of it this way. Just as a heart surgeon must first discover the source of a problem—blockages, leaky valves, circuitry issues, or any number of potential problems—so we must identify the root of our heartaches so that we can surrender our hearts fully to the Great Physician for some spiritual heart surgery. As we take the time to allow God to work in our hearts, we will spend less time trying to diagnose and fix the hearts of those around us.

Let's be honest. Most of us spend much more time evaluating the hearts of others than we do our own. In fact, we're experts at it. We read into every word, expression, and body language cue to form a conclusion about how the other person feels and thinks, and we may be off course. With other people's parenting, finances, and even their marriages, we are quick to see where they are wrong. While sometimes the Lord leads us to address the actions of others privately if we see them clearly sinning (Matthew 18), we must be sure we aren't making assumptions or deciding their motives. For example, I've heard others say they know another is judging them or thinking bad thoughts about them. Another way we judge others' hearts is to read an alternate message into a comment or gesture. We write a story in our mind deciding what they must be feeling and thinking and usually it is not good. No one can truly know what is in the heart of another because none of us really knows what it is like to be in their head or have all their experiences.

The reality is that focusing on others' heart issues only wastes our time and distracts us from dealing with our own heart issues—which is what really needs our attention. When we actually spend our mental and emotional energy allowing God to evaluate the sin in our hearts first, we usually find that we see others and their situations differently. By being aware of our personal tendencies toward sin and expending our time and energy on our own repentance, we can view others with more grace and less judgment. And that frees us to love them with a heart that overflows with God's love. We can look at them the way that God sees them—valuable and worth sending Jesus to die for them.

Let's ask God to help us understand our feelings, seek wise counsel to draw out our heart issues (see Proverbs 20:5), and repent and confess to our loving Father the wickedness hidden in our hearts. He already knows anyway, and He wants us to acknowledge it so that He can renew and transform us. Our loving Father offers us new hearts, but first we must surrender our sinful ones to Him. God says He searches and examines our secret motives, and this is a very good thing! Even though the process can be painful, it opens us to seeing where our hearts have begun to harden so that God's healing work can begin.

In addition to asking questions about our hearts, it can be helpful to evaluate the climate of our hearts, which can sometimes fluctuate like the temperature on a thermometer. We read about the fluctuating climate or condition of the human heart in God's Word from Genesis to Revelation. Take a moment and see how many of these descriptions of the heart resonated with your personal heart climate over the last week:

A heavy heart can be
anguished (Psalm 38:8);
bitter (Psalm 73:21; Proverbs 14:10);
broken (Genesis 6:6; Psalm 42:4; 69:20);
carrying the insults of others (Psalm 89:50);
crooked (Proverbs 11:20);
cursing God (Job 1:5);

deceived (Deuteronomy 11:16);
doubting (Luke 24:38);
dull and stupid (Psalm 119:70);
evil, wicked (Psalm 28:3; Proverbs 26:23);
fearful (Joshua 2:11);
fickle (Hosea 10:2);
full of pain (Psalm 109:22);
hard (Exodus 4:21; too many references to list);
hateful (Leviticus 19:17);
heavy (Proverbs 14:13; Isaiah 24:16);
hypocritical (Matthew 23:28);
like wax, melting within me (Psalm 22:14);
lying (Jeremiah 14:14);
overwhelmed (Psalm 61:2);
perverted (Proverbs 6:14);
proud (Proverbs 21:4; Ezekiel 28:17);
sad (Psalm 13:2; 42:5);
sick (Job 23:16; Psalm 102:4; Isaiah 1:5);
stubborn (Exodus 7:3);
troubled and restless (Job 30:27); or
turned away from the Lord (1 Kings 11:9; Psalm 95:10; Jeremiah 17:5).

A soft heart can be
able to change (Deuteronomy 10:16);
believing (Romans 10:9-10);
clean (Psalm 51:10);
compassionate (Luke 7:13);
fully committed to God (2 Chronicles 16:9; Psalm 125:4);
generous (Exodus 35:5);

gentle (Matthew 11:29);
glad (Psalm 16:9);
happy, cheerful (Proverbs 15:15; 17:22);
honest (Psalm 36:10);
humble and contrite (Isaiah 66:2);
loving (Deuteronomy 6:5);
new (1 Samuel 10:9);
open (2 Corinthians 6:11);
peaceful (Proverbs 14:30; John 14:27);
prayerful (Genesis 24:45; Psalm 119:145);
pure (Psalm 24:4; 73:1);
rejoicing (1 Samuel 2:1);
repentant (Psalm 51:17; Isaiah 57:15);
responsive (Ezekiel 36:26);
searching, seeking God (Deuteronomy 4:29;
  1 Chronicles 22:19);
sincere (Psalm 15:2);
thankful (Colossians 3:16);
true and right (Psalm 7:10; 97:11);
understanding (1 Kings 3:9; Proverbs 14:33);
undivided (2 Chronicles 19:9; Ezekiel 11:19);
virtuous (Psalm 94:15); or
willing (Exodus 35:22; 2 Chronicles 29:31).

Were you able to identify with these descriptions of your own heart? Did you find yourself relating to those in the first category or the second? In any given week I can go from wearing the insults of others and feeling overwhelmed or fearful to finding that God is transforming my heart with love and peace. Here's some very good news: God cares more about the condition of our hearts than almost anything else. Jesus said in Luke 6:45b, "What you say from what is in your heart." We serve a God who not only looks at our hearts but also wants us to pour out our hearts to Him. He invites us to get real about our joys and pains. We don't have to hide in shame; we can acknowledge our fluctuating feelings and know that He wants to help us down the path of self-discovery that leads to healing.

Seeing our hearts the way God sees them is our first step in keeping our hearts soft. Like David teaches us in Psalm 139, it is good to wait in God's presence, asking Him to search our hearts and help us see where change is needed. This can make for a time of conviction, confession, and repentance—but that is when real heart change can happen.

Behavior Modification vs. Heart Change

After taking some time to evaluate our hearts, our tendency is to go into "change my behavior mode." We say to ourselves, "Okay, now that I see the hardness, bitterness, and deception in my heart, I will get up every day and do my quiet time, go to church every Sunday (even when I'm tired), and try to watch less TV. That should help change my heart." However, when we over-concentrate on actions, we end up like the Pharisees in the New Testament who followed rules meticulously but had hearts filled with wrong motives. It was to them that Jesus quoted the prophet Isaiah: "These people honor me with their lips, / but their hearts are far from me" (Matthew 15:8). Jeremiah's statement was similar: "Your name is on their lips, / but you are far from their hearts" (Jeremiah 12:2b). God wants us to honor Him not only with our actions but also with the motives of our hearts.

When we look into our hearts deeply and see the deceitfulness, self-preservation, and selfishness there, we need to be careful not to try to fix ourselves. It's dangerous to become like the Pharisees and try to follow rules in an attempt to clean up our hearts. That is not what God has in mind. Heart change happens internally first and then displays itself externally as we acknowledge and respond to the sin we've identified.

In Jeremiah 3:12-25, God calls His people to take some steps once they've evaluated their hearts and found them hardened by sin. Basically, he calls them to *know it*, *share it*, and *own it*. This message, which is clearly laid out in this passage, is found throughout Scripture. Let's consider these three steps together.

1. Know It

Sometimes it can be scary to admit how we feel. At times I get angry at my children, am reluctant to forgive my husband, or feel jealous of my friends. I would rather pretend that I am naturally kind, forgiving, and content; but in reality, my heart "default" usually starts me in the opposite direction. In order to become more like Christ, I first must be honest about the struggle. Because God promises to be merciful, we can abandon our pride and come clean about our tendency to sin. When we evaluate our hearts, we then have the choice to ignore our heart tendencies or admit them. Jeremiah 3:13a instructs us, "Only acknowledge your guilt. / Admit that you rebelled against the LORD your God." Being honest with ourselves is a necessary first step. One thing that helps me to "know it" is to use the list of heart descriptions on the preceding pages. By going through some biblical descriptions of hearts, I can find a few words to encapsulate what seems to be going on in my own heart. As I tell God what is going on in my heart, it helps me to identify and embrace what I'm asking Him to transform inside of me.

2. Share It

After we acknowledge to ourselves the sin in our hearts, then we move on to sharing the truth with God and others. Of course, God already knows our sin, but He asks us to share it with Him for the sake of our relationship.

When our children come to us with the story of something that has happened, we listen to hear their perspective, even if we have observed with our own eyes everything they have done. This allows us to experience the event together, whether we are celebrating or mourning. At a recent wedding of a family friend, I enjoyed hearing how my daughters experienced it even though we were all together. They noticed things I didn't, recalled funny moments on the dance floor (where I was not participating), and chose a different flavor of cake than the one I had devoured. In the same way, sharing our joys and pains with God brings us closer to Him.

In Jeremiah 3:13b we read, "Confess that you refused to listen to my voice. / I, the Lord, have spoken!" The original Hebrew word used for the verb "confess" is *shama*. As we saw in the previous chapter, *shama* usually means to "hear with attention or interest," but it also can mean "to cause to hear, tell, proclaim; to make proclamation."[1] Although most times in Jeremiah *shama* is translated "hear" or "listen," in this passage it is usually translated "confess" or "obey." Once we know our sin, we need to confess it to God—and possibly others if our heart attitudes have caused them pain.

Though we always should confess our sin to God, the decision to share with others must be led by the Holy Spirit. Sometimes our sin is between us and God alone. Perhaps others are not directly impacted or the situation does not require an outward confession. Other times we need to go and repent to those impacted by our sin. As we seek God's guidance, the Holy Spirit will give us clarity about whether we need to confess to God alone or to both God and others.

I remember a humbling experience when I had the opportunity to do this. Just as Job's friends made assumptions about his guilt, I did a similar thing by taking out my "microscope" to examine another person's motives. Regrettably, I also discussed the situation with her in a public place in front of our children. Not a good idea. I was defensive and said things that couldn't be retracted. Like a tube of toothpaste, I squeezed the words out, and there was no way to stuff them back in. It took some time to work through my emotions and justifications, but later as I was able to evaluate my own heart from God's perspective and see my sin, He prompted me to go to her. I repented of my poor decisions and apologized for hurting her with my words and actions. Sharing my heart of ownership and regret brought us closer and took us down a path of reconciliation.

I'm thankful that God wants us to be honest about our hearts—with Him and with others—so that He can create newness there. Just as we must admit our symptoms to a doctor, who then can prescribe the right treatment, so we must admit our heart troubles to the Great Physician, who knows the cure. Only then are we in a position to follow His treatment of repentance and confession.

I don't know about you, but confessing my sin to others ranks low on my favorite activities list. For me, it's right up there with trips to the dentist, cleaning the toilets, and changing dirty diapers (which, thankfully, I only do occasionally now when babysitting for friends). I often dread it even though I know it needs to be done. It can be humbling if not downright humiliating. Confessing our sin exposes our deceitful hearts. However, James tells us a great benefit of this kind of vulnerable sharing: "Confess your sins to each other and pray for each other *so that you may be healed*. The earnest prayer of a righteous person has great power and produces wonderful results" (5:16, emphasis added). Power and wonderful results—sounds good to me!

Yet all too often we miss out on this healing in the body of Christ. Many of us walk around "bleeding" from the wounds of our fellow believers. God wants to heal our relational strife, but we must be willing to humbly confess our part.

You may be saying, "But I did nothing wrong. I am the offended party. The other person needs to come and confess to me." There are times when we have been mistreated and we truly are innocent victims, such as in cases of abuse. This is not what I am talking about here. Those situations require no repentance on our part but instead the healing work of God in our hearts, most often through forgiveness. In all other instances of relational strife, we must be willing to admit and confess our sin.

The people of Judah were unwilling to humbly confess their sin. They had a self-righteous posture, believing they had done nothing wrong. I have been there in my thinking as well when relational friction has occurred. Not only is this kind of self-deception dangerous to ourselves, it often leads us to strike back. When someone hurts us, it is the nature of our deceitful hearts to want to hurt back, whether overtly or covertly. To retaliate, we might judge, gossip, ignore, or build up high walls that say "keep out" to those who have hurt us. In one way or another, we often end up sinning. Even if the other person has 90 percent to confess and we have only 10 percent, we can share that 10 percent and humbly ask for forgiveness.

So let me ask you: Is there anyone you need to confess sin to, so that healing can begin? It may even be sin the other person doesn't even know you've been harboring in your heart. If the Holy Spirit brought someone to mind, I challenge you to put James 5:16 into practice and confess your sin, trusting the Holy Spirit to guard your heart. If the person is local, no texting, e-mail, or phone calls allowed; do it face-to-face so that they can see your facial expression and body language as well as hear your words. This will give the best possible chance for clear communication and reconciliation.

3. Own It

Once we have admitted our sin to ourselves and confessed our sin to God and others, we then must take personal responsibility for our actions. When you approach a brother or sister in Christ to confess your sin, be sure that you own it. Don't say, "The devil made me do it," give three reasons why your sin was justified, or point out their own failings. That is blaming, not taking personal responsibility.

Blame is an epidemic in our culture. It's much easier to pass the buck or create excuses to validate bad decisions. Yet God says it's better to just own it. No excuses. No blaming. Just say, "I thought/said/did this, and I am sorry."

Perhaps you're concerned that taking personal responsibility for sin might trap you in a cycle of shame or self-deprecation. Actually, owning your sin will take you to a place of freedom because Jesus has already paid the price for it. He lifts our shame when we admit our sin and give it to Him. First John 1:9 assures us of this truth: "But if we confess our sins to him, he is faithful and just to forgive us our sins and to cleanse us from all wickedness." Confession is the path to healing, not condemnation.

What we see in Jeremiah 3:25 is a call to own it:

> "Let us now lie down in shame
> and cover ourselves with dishonor,
> for we and our ancestors have sinned
> against the LORD our God.
> From our childhood to this day
> we have never obeyed him."

This is not a call to remain in shame and reproach but to allow godly sorrow to move us to repentance. Only then can we revel in our God who forgives and heals. Rather than viewing God as a shame-giver in this verse, we should focus on His character as a merciful Father who grieves to watch His children running down a destructive road. God does not want us to feel bad about ourselves but, rather, to feel grief over our destructive choices and behaviors. He wants us to acknowledge our guilt because He knows that this is the path to forgiveness, freedom, and life.

This same verse uses the Hebrew word *chaciyd* (also *chasid*, *hasid*) in referring to God. It is a term that means "faithful, kind, godly, holy one, saint, pious."[2] Earlier in Jeremiah 3 we read, "For I am merciful," says the Lord (v. 12). The Old Testament gets a bad reputation for portraying God as militant and full of judgment. Yet what we see here is the God who is the same yesterday, today, and forever. He may go to great lengths to bring us back to Him in ways we can't always understand, but His mercy is always present. We can know, share, and own our sin because God in His mercy will forgive and help us turn from it. He doesn't ask us to clean ourselves up, fix our bad behavior, and then approach Him. No! He welcomes us *in our brokenness*. Our merciful, faithful God is the only One who can change our hearts.

So what is our part? Simply to hand over the pride and power in our hearts, yielding them to God. Changing our hearts doesn't mean deciding to change our actions in our own strength. If we try that, we will fail every time. I know; I've tried. We have to come to God in our weakness and surrender because we are at the end of ourselves. That's when God's power works best.

King David is a great example of someone who understood surrender and chose to know it, share it, and own it in regard to his sin. He is called a man after God's heart because he understood that only God could help him with his sin problem. This is his prayer in Psalm 51:9-10:

> Don't keep looking at my sins.
> Remove the stain of my guilt.
> Create in me a clean heart, O God.
> Renew a loyal spirit within me.

David didn't say, "God, I know I've done wrong, so here is my plan to do everything right from now on." Rather, he recognized his inability to fix his own heart through behavior modification and his need to surrender.

Let's stop trying to do in our human strength the work that God alone can do, and let's let go of pride and surrender to God so that He can change our hearts. Even in our worst moments—those times when we have yielded to the same temptation yet again—He calls us to come. Our tendency to hide in shame started back in the garden with the very first sin, yet God still seeks us out. He never forces us to follow but waits and calls to us, offering mercy and hope. And all we have to do is run into His outstretched arms—knowing, sharing, and owning how very much we need Him. He can handle it, no matter how broken our hearts may be!

Where Do Broken Hearts Go

Hearts are fragile. In the physical realm, heart disease is the leading cause of death for men and women in America. *Blood pressure, blockages, attacks, aneurysms, leaking valves, irregular beats,* and *angina* are just a few of the terms describing things that can go wrong with our hearts. In the spiritual realm, the list is even longer for the potential problems with our hearts. Just take another look at the list on pages 106–108, which is only a fraction of those we find in Scripture.

The pages of Jeremiah show us a prophecy of what lies ahead for the people of Judah because of the problems with their hearts, and it's not a pretty picture. He even likens their fear and anguish to that of a woman in labor. I don't know about you, but to me that sounds like severe anguish!

Finding out I was having twins just ten days before I had them caused great fear in this gal who'd already experienced the birth of a singleton. I knew what to expect. The thought of doubling that encounter freaked me right out. Sometimes our trials are not physical experiences, such as birthing a child, but are emotional, mental, and spiritual labors. Such trials are able to birth great intimacy with Christ, but the process can be excruciating.

God tells us to mourn like the loss of an only son. He knew even then that He would be offering up Jesus as a sacrifice. Anguish and pain are not foreign to our God. He designed our frame and knows we need to express our emotions when we are hurting instead of bottling them up like our "grin and bear it" culture encourages. Eastern culture diametrically opposes Western practices when it comes to grieving. In fact, in biblical times they even hired mourners when someone died, as we see in the Gospels when Jesus was called in to heal.

Today we live like ducks on the water—looking cool and collected above the water line while underneath it's paddle, paddle, paddle. And sometimes we can feel like we're paddling without an oar! The strength of the current causes us to paddle like crazy, and it seems we aren't getting anywhere. We often find ourselves with spiritual "chest pain" from all this paddling. Friends betray us. Our children speak hurtful words. Coworkers treat us badly. Relationships wound us. Then there are circumstances that cause us pain. We lose our jobs. Finances are tight. Divorce papers are filed. Life is hard!

Jesus warned us it would be this way in John 16:33: "I have told you all this so that you may have peace in me. Here on earth you will have many trials and sorrows. But take heart, because I have overcome the world." We know that Jesus is the Overcomer, so why do we bring Him our broken hearts only after we've tried everything else to fix them? We call a friend or family member. We try to manage and manipulate the circumstances. We numb ourselves with a quick fix—food, shopping, television. Anything to try to fix it ourselves. But nothing ever really works.

The Israelites did the same thing. They had tough circumstances. They were facing invasions, poverty, and deportation from the only home they'd ever known. Instead of turning to the Lord of Heaven's Armies, they tried idol worship, political negotiations, and anything else they could think of. They lacked faith in God's power to really do something. And as hard as it may be to admit, that's really what it boils down to with us too.

If you find yourself resistant to the idea that you may lack faith in God, just ask yourself these questions: *What is the very first thing I do when I'm upset about something? Where do I turn instantly?* God calls us to be careful to turn to Him *first*, to bring our hurting hearts to Him before taking action ourselves or seeking the help or advice of others. Only He can heal us and use our pain and sorrow to refine us, and He promises to purify us through our trials—if we will yield to the process. Unfortunately, Judah had a stubborn streak for idolatry and independence that didn't fare well in the fire.

Fire is a purifying agent. In Jeremiah 6:27, God says to Jeremiah, "I have made you a tester of metals, / that you may determine the quality of my people." Using Jeremiah's illustration, our quality of metal is revealed through the fire. If God's people are not purified by fire, He will label them "rejected silver." Or here's another visual. I'm a tea drinker, so every morning I pour boiling water over a bag of tea. The tiny leaves inside that bag are permeated by the water, staining it dark brown and flavoring it. Similarly, who we really are inside comes out when the "hot water" of life scalds us.

When the fires or scalding waters of life come, we need to be daring with hope in God rather than turning to other things to numb our pain. If we will bring our hurting hearts to Christ first, He can use our pain to refine and shape us so that we don't become like rejected silver or discarded tea leaves. God wants us to allow Him to do a deep work in us by developing our character through trials and difficulties, but He will never force our hands. The people of Judah chose rebellion and wickedness, and their problems made their hearts harder until seventy years of captivity finally convinced them to submit to God's ways.

How about you? Are you learning from your trials, or are you giving yourself permission to gossip, slander, and lead others into sin because of your pain? What comes out when the hot water of life is poured over you?

In this world we will have trouble, but we can choose to bring our troubles to the One who has overcome this world—our great God! God doesn't want us to ignore our problems, stuff our feelings, or pretend we aren't hurting. He wants us to come to Him, surrender our hearts, and trust Him even when we can't see Him and our lives seem to be falling apart. This is what it means to dare to hope in an unstable world.

Go to God with your heart burdens. You can trust Him with your broken heart. He will not only heal your heart, He will teach you how to guard it.

Guard Your Heart

A dear friend called one day to tell me about an encounter she had with her fourteen-year-old son. They were camping for the weekend, and she woke up one morning with a vivid memory of her dream. In the dream the family was driving in their van, and her son used some foul language. No one corrected him or showed any surprise at his inappropriate words. They all just went on with conversation as usual. She heard God's Spirit speak to her that her son was losing his shock factor. His exposure to bad language through school and sports was starting to desensitize him. She hadn't heard him use these words, but it was clear they needed to have a talk.

As they were driving home from camping, she had her other children ride with their father so she could have some time alone with her son. She told him, "I know you're struggling with bad language." His eyes looked like they were about to pop out of his skull. "How did you know?" he responded. "God told me in a dream," she said. His eyes were popping out even farther now. My friend took a few minutes to explain what happens when we don't guard our hearts. We lose our shock factor. She explained that it's like when a frog is put into a pot of lukewarm water and the heat is slowly turned up. The frog won't jump out even when the water boils because the temperature slowly creeps up on him until it's too late. She encouraged her son not to let this happen with his words.

The Israelites in Jeremiah's day had also lost their shock factor. Jeremiah repeats a word picture over and over to describe their condition: he says that they have forgotten how to blush (6:15; 8:12). Israel forgot how to blush. God wants us to blush over our sin and then repent. This kind of conviction that leads to repentance is sometimes referred to as healthy shame.

In her book *Shame Lifter*, Marilyn Hontz writes, "Healthy shame ought to lead us toward repentance and restoration, healing and forgiveness."[3] Healthy shame is not to be confused with the toxic shame that comes from the enemy who leads us to feelings of worthlessness and judgment. God never wants us to live in a place of hopelessness paralyzed with feelings of failure. While that kind of shame is the enemy's game, the conviction of the Holy Spirit is intended to help us guard our hearts and protect them.

Why do our hearts need to be guarded? Because God desires us to lead pure lives. You might say that guarding our hearts helps us to keep blushing as we should.

We have to be careful about what we allow to influence our hearts. What goes into, or influences, our hearts directly affects what comes out of our hearts. As we saw earlier, Jesus said, "What you say flows from what is in your heart" (Luke 6:45b). So by guarding our hearts, we also are guarding what comes out of our mouths. One of the best ways to guard our hearts is to guard our minds, because heart attitudes are largely determined by our thoughts.

Jeremiah often warned the people about their thought lives and words:

> O Jerusalem, cleanse your heart
>   that you may be saved.
> How long will you harbor
>   your evil thoughts?
>
> (Jeremiah 4:14)

> "But I will be merciful only if you stop your evil thoughts and deeds and start treating each other with justice." (Jeremiah 7:5)

Guarding our hearts means using caution about what we allow to influence our thoughts, words, and actions. It doesn't mean we close ourselves off from difficult people or painful circumstances. It also doesn't mean we totally isolate ourselves from our culture. Instead, we must figure out how to live in this world without allowing our hearts to become attached to it.

Take a moment to consider your own thought life. Do you allow yourself to think about things you shouldn't, dwell on others' faults, or let bitterness, envy, or worry creep in? What about your words? Have you lost your shock factor—not just in foul language but also in regard to gossip, disrespect, reckless speech, or angry words? Are the majority of your words helpful to those who hear them?

In a world that offers easy and instant access to an overwhelming amount of information and stimuli, guarding our hearts takes great intentionality. With remotes, keyboards, and touch screens increasing our exposure to harmful influences, we can easily become desensitized. God longs for us to keep our hearts soft so that we are grieved when inappropriate behaviors are considered acceptable. He asks us to guard what we allow to flow both in and out of our hearts. Allowing the Holy Spirit and God's Word to be our "filter" helps keep our words and actions from damaging our hearts as well as the hearts of those around us. And guarding our hearts in this way frees us to give God our whole hearts.

With All Your Heart

Have you ever heard John Mayer's song "Half of My Heart"? There was a time several years ago when I heard this song regularly in my morning aerobics class. The song has stuck in my mind because in it Mayer laments how he finds it hard to love with only half of his heart, yet he says this is all he can seem to give. He basically says that he is too selfish to give his girlfriend his whole heart, admitting he's a man who has "never truly loved anything."

I've thought often about those lyrics, which are reminiscent of a mega theme in God's Word. Over and over God talks about those who were half-hearted in their pursuit of Him (such as Saul and Solomon) and those who had a whole heart for God (such as David and Joseph). Scripture is clear: God doesn't want half of our hearts; He wants us to give Him our *whole* hearts!

So often we're like the Israelites in Jeremiah's day, who gave God their leftovers. In Jeremiah 24 we read about a vision Jeremiah had of two baskets of figs—one filled with fresh, ripe figs and the other filled with rotten figs. The figs in this vision were located at the front of the Temple, which is where the people brought their offerings to the Lord. They were supposed to give God their firstfruits, the best of what they harvested. But as the vision reveals, when people lost faith in God's power, and perhaps even His very existence, they kept the best for themselves and put their rotten leftovers in the offering baskets at the Temple.

Similarly, our offerings to God reveal what we really believe about Him. We may attend church sporadically, say prayers at dinner, and do just enough to assuage our conscience and help us feel "spiritual enough"; but often we put more time and intentionality into planning our next vacation or our children's birthday parties and keeping up with our work and school schedules than we do intensely pursuing God with our whole hearts. We neglect God's Word and prayer, and we can't remember the last time we shared our faith. While offering God our leftovers, we wonder why we often seem to be losing the spiritual battle against sin and the enemy in our lives. And just to be clear, I'm including myself in this *we*!

We all desperately need to pursue God with our whole hearts, remembering the words of Ephesians 5:15-17: "So be careful how you live. Don't live like fools, but like those who are wise. Make the most of every opportunity in these evil days. Don't act thoughtlessly, but understand what the Lord wants you to do." God wants nothing less than for us to live a sold-out, on-fire, radical, wholehearted life in deep relationship with Him.

King Zedekiah teaches us about being half-hearted. If we look throughout Jeremiah's prophecy, we find a great contrast between Zedekiah's life and Jeremiah's life. Zedekiah didn't listen to God, tried to solve his problems through political alliances, cared more about what others thought of him than what God thought, allowed fear of surrender to matter more than God, and was a coward. On the other hand, Jeremiah listened to God, preached that victory comes through

We need to remember that our faithful God offers us hope and healing as we surrender our broken hearts to Him.

surrender to God, cared more about God than what others thought, obeyed God wholeheartedly even if it brought struggle, and followed God no matter what.

When we look at this contrast in print, it's easy to want to have a whole heart for God. But when difficulty and struggle come, clinging to what we cannot see and having faith to obey God's counterculture message is tougher than it sounds. Sometimes it's just easier to trust in tangible things such as people, money, and human effort, right? So what are we to do? We must look beyond the tangible to the intangible, remembering what we've been designed for.

God created us for fullness of life; and although sin has marred God's original design, He has redeemed us through Christ. God doesn't desire all of our hearts because He is possessive or controlling; He simply knows that we are designed for intimacy with Him. He knows that our half-hearted attempts at following Him will lead only to dissatisfaction, complacency, and mediocrity—leaving us wanting something more. When we don't find our satisfaction in God, we tend to look to empty substitutes that can never satisfy. So God calls us to wholehearted devotion, and He leads us by His own example—not sparing His only Son to show us His whole-hearted affection.

Dealing with our heart issues isn't easy. Many of us have been hurt deeply by others, whether through abuse, neglect, or rejection. Others of us may not have suffered as much, but we still need to work through the daily wear and tear on our hearts as we live in a fallen world. In either case, we need to remember that our faithful God offers us hope and healing as we surrender our broken hearts to Him. God calls us to trust Him and dare to hope in Him—even with the most fragile of hearts.

Dare to Hope Challenge

In order to be intentional about giving your heart fully to God, I invite you to seal these five "heart cautions" in your mind—and maybe even write them down. Then rehearse them regularly as a heart checkup that will help you to give your whole heart to God:

1. Be careful to evaluate your own heart.
2. Be careful not to confuse behavior modification with heart change.
3. Be careful to bring your hurting heart to God.
4. Be careful to guard your heart.
5. Be careful to seek God wholeheartedly.

Whenever you rehearse these "heart cautions," be sure to take time in God's presence, letting Him speak His whole-hearted love over *you*—His dearly loved child. Never forget that God loves you with all of His heart!

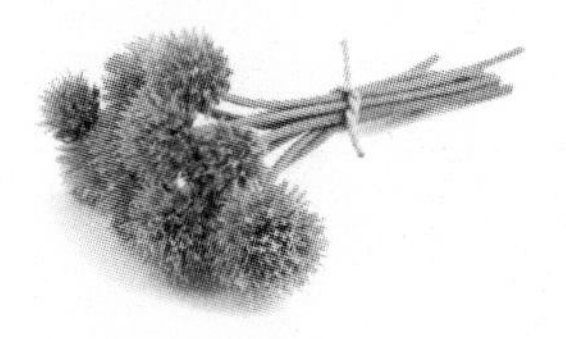

CHAPTER 5

Quitting the Blame Game

Take Personal Responsibility

This is what the Lord says:
"Don't let the wise boast in their wisdom,
or the powerful boast in their power,
or the rich boast in their riches.
But those who wish to boast
should boast in this alone:
that they truly know me and understand that I am the Lord."

—Jeremiah 9:23-24

I love being a parent. Though I now have three kids in college and only one living at home, I still enjoy spending time with all of my kids. Of course, there have been plenty of challenges along the way, including conflicts among siblings. When it comes to those conflicts, the thing that gets under my skin the most is blaming. I remember the days when all four were living at home like it was yesterday. One sibling would say that another sibling was to blame for his or her failure to complete a chore or make a wise choice. Then when I investigated and pointed out the blaming child's own sin or failure in the situation, the blame could quickly turn to me. I would be told that I made unfair decisions, expected too much, or didn't understand them. My discipline or consequences were viewed as measures to "ruin their lives." Over and over I tried to explain that if I didn't care, I wouldn't take the time and energy to correct, train, pray, and discipline. (Anyone nodding in solidarity right now?) It's a wonderful thing to begin to see the fruit of that discipline as they are growing into adulthood.

Proverbs says that parents who don't love their children fail to discipline them (13:24). Likewise, God's love is what motivates His discipline in our lives—including when we don't take personal responsibility but play the blame game. And yes, blame is something we still struggle with as adults—sometimes even without our full awareness. But as we'll see in this chapter, we can find help for quitting this destructive "game" in the Book of Jeremiah.

God's Good Discipline

A helpful first step toward quitting the blame game is to surrender to God's good discipline in our lives, and this requires understanding God's character—that He is always loving, holding mercy and justice in perfect balance. The many passages in Jeremiah that include God's judgment can fly in the face of our theology of God's love and mercy, but God's justice and mercy actually hold hands as He disciplines us like a good father. Let's look together at two of the loving benefits of God's good discipline that we find in Jeremiah 12.

1. Right Perspective

As we've seen repeatedly, Jeremiah was much like us. His prophet status did not exempt him from making complaints and asking honest questions. He struggled with the same questions I sometimes have: Why do the wicked prosper? Why are evil people happy? But Jeremiah knew just where to take questions such as these, and he teaches us that God can handle our questions.

In Jeremiah 12:2 we learn that the wicked but happy people Jeremiah was referring to were not those of the surrounding pagan nations but those who had God's name on their lips though their hearts were a million miles away. He wrote,

> You have planted them,
> and they have taken root and prospered.

> Your name is on their lips,
> but you are far from their hearts.

Jeremiah sacrificed everything in his pursuit of God. He lost the approval of his family, his safety, and his status in society; God even instructed him not to marry and have children. Yet those around him who were speaking God's name but not living the life to back up their words seemed to be happy, healthy, and living the good life. We often see the same thing happening today. When we take bold steps of faith, complications can face us at every turn. Yet we look at those around us who appear to be living for themselves and loving it. From our viewpoint, it just isn't fair. Doing the right thing doesn't seem to bring the benefits it should.

God allows our questions about this seeming injustice, but He also helps us get some much-needed perspective on our situation. By verse 5, God responds to Jeremiah's questions:

> "If racing against mere men makes you tired,
> how will you race against horses?
> If you stumble and fall on open ground,
> what will you do in the thickets near the Jordan?
> Even your brothers, members of your own family,
> have turned against you.
> They plot and raise complaints against you.
> Do not trust them,
> no matter how pleasantly they speak. (vv. 5-6)

In other words, "If you think this is tough or unfair, brace yourself. Transfer your trust from any person or thing to My care, or the ride ahead may be rocky!" God is not threatening us in any way but warning us to continually trust in His sovereignty because He knows the dangers of reverting to our human strength. This message echoes the theme of idolatry we explored in chapter 2. When we believe our security is found in relationships, status, possessions, or anything else, God is willing to allow the ground beneath our feet to shake in order to see if we remember where our true foundation lies. As the old hymn "My Hope Is Built" reminds us, "On Christ the solid rock I stand, all other ground is sinking sand."[1]

In verse 5 God essentially asks Jeremiah, "If you are perplexed when phony people appear to be happy, then what will you do when your own brothers turn against you?" Ouch. I've experienced some testing of my own places where I turn to find security. Though I claim God as my safe place, ugly idols can creep in, trying to usurp the number one place in my life. There have been times in my life when healthy relationships quickly became harmful because I held them too tightly. Have you ever had that experience? This is where devoted God-followers are separated from those who are just giving God lip service. If racing against people makes us tired, then we won't fare well in the horse race if we attempt to run in our own strength.

God was cautioning Jeremiah through these two physical illustrations, reminding him where he should put his hope and confidence. We can sum it up in three words: *Trust Me alone.*

I have learned this the hard way. When I have gotten into the mind-set that life just isn't fair and traveled down a path of "woe is me" thinking, God has said to me through these verses in Jeremiah, "If you think this situation is hard, dig up your tree and plant it a little closer to the riverbank. Don't put your hope in people or fleeting circumstancial ease; don't trust anyone or anything but Me."

Of course, God wants us to live in community and to have friends and family. He isn't calling us to put up huge walls around our hearts and shut everyone out. The issue here is where our ultimate "safe place" resides. If we elevate anything or anyone above God in our lives, we will find our perspective of justice becomes warped. Without exception, when we look to people or circumstances to find our identity, they will ultimately fail to fill our God-shaped hole. So whenever we feel this emptiness, we must be careful to trust God instead of trying to figure out what is "fair" and "unfair" according to our limited view.

2. The Principle of Sowing and Reaping

Another benefit of God's good discipline is understanding the principle of sowing and reaping, which we find in the second half of Jeremiah 12.

After God settles the trust issue, He goes on to explain Himself briefly, giving Jeremiah a little sneak peek into the journey ahead. In verses 2-13 of Jeremiah 12, God speaks of the future events that are coming for the people of Judah. These are the same people Jeremiah is whining about who seem to be sinning with no consequences. God says they will be destroyed by surrounding nations. The Lord reminds Jeremiah and the people that while it can seem like no consequences are happening, they can rest assured that they will reap what they are sowing.

I am grateful God doesn't always give me this kind of glimpse! I'm glad He didn't spell out to me in high school all the details of what lay ahead for me. So much of it has been thrilling, but the details of childbirth, sickness, heartbreak, cross-country moves, and raising teenagers were better left to tackle as they came. Sometimes it's easier to take life one day at a time. Amen? No need for sneak peeks. Yet as

God's prophet to Judah, Jeremiah has the coming destruction spelled out for him, and it doesn't look good.

In verse 13, God says that the people planted wheat but harvested thorns and that they will harvest a crop of shame. Here we see a principle found throughout God's Word: sowing and reaping. Galatians 6:7 says that "God is not mocked, for you reap whatever you sow" (NRSV). When we plant seeds of rebellion, closed ears, and idolatry, we reap a harvest of shame and consequences. The people of Judah found this out the hard way: they lived it.

We need this reminder about sowing and reaping so that when we read the passages in Jeremiah about the harsh realities of war, exile, and poverty that God allowed the Israelites living in Judah to experience, we don't become like them and view God as unfair, unwilling, and unloving. These aren't passages we should be embarrassed about or want to hide in favor of New Testament verses about love and grace. God's message of love is consistent throughout the Scriptures, including these passages in Jeremiah about God's discipline.

Yet still we struggle to understand all the hardship and suffering in the world. I mean, surely sowing and reaping doesn't cover all of that. Why *does* God allow difficulty or suffering in our lives—in *your* life?

I wish there was a neat, easy answer for this question. But there are no easy answers when it comes to suffering, and beware of anyone who says otherwise. Volumes have been written on the question of suffering by experts in many disciplines, including scholars, theologians, pastors, psychologists, physicians, and others. I cannot begin to adequately explore the depths of the subject here. But to give us some needed context for our discussion of God's good discipline regarding sowing and reaping, let's broaden our focus for a moment and briefly consider three general categories of suffering.

1. We suffer because we live in a fallen, sinful world. After Eve and Adam ate the forbidden fruit, sin entered the world. As a result, disease, violence, and the wrong choices made by others affect us just because we live on this planet. Romans 8:20 says, "Against its will, all creation was subjected to God's curse." Much of our suffering is the result of being born into a world marked by sin—from the weeds in our gardens to the pain of childbirth and the many other effects of the rebellion back in Genesis. Much of the suffering we experience personally as well as what we watch on the nightly news falls into this category, including but not limited to medical conditions, diseases, accidents, violence, senseless tragedies, and natural disasters.

2. Other times we suffer because of our obedience to God. Jeremiah followed God wholeheartedly and yet he was beaten, put in chains, jailed, and lowered into a mud-filled cistern to die. These trials were not consequences of bad decisions—they did not fall into the category of sowing and reaping. Rather, they were the result of living in a sinful world that is hostile to the things of God. Yet instead of moping and blaming God (okay, Jeremiah did do a little moping; see 20:14-18), Jeremiah trusted God. Even if his rescue wouldn't come until the next life, he put his trust in the Lord of Heaven's Armies, and God sustained Jeremiah through the difficulties. Paul says in 2 Timothy 3:12 that this kind of suffering will be our experience as well: "Yes, and everyone who wants to live a godly life in Christ Jesus will suffer persecution." Our persecution may not include physical hardship, but following God's way will include some pushback and even hostility from others at times. When coworkers make fun of us for our faith or we are left out of a social gathering because of our moral standards, we get a taste of what it means to suffer because of our obedience.

3. Suffering can also be the result of bad choices that we make. Here's where the principle of reaping and sowing comes into play. When we overspend habitually, we can't be mad at God because we can't pay our bills. When we choose to treat our bodies, God's temple, with neglect from habitual unhealthy eating, poor sleeping habits, and lack of exercise, we can't blame God for the related health problems. When we live on a spiritual diet of TV, magazines, media, gossip, and other soul junk food, we can't blame God that we don't experience victory over sin. When we neglect to take the time to prayerfully discipline our children, there are sure to be consequences. I'm sure you could name other examples. The list could go on and on!

But here's the good news when it comes to sowing and reaping—to our bad choices that yield bad results. Our God is a good Daddy, and He will use anything to get His children's attention when we are making terrible decisions. God will allow us to suffer the consequences of our bad choices if that's what it takes to bring us back into relationship with Him. Just as we must allow discomfort in our children's lives when they rebel, disobey, and make unwise choices, God is the perfect parent in our lives, allowing us to reap what we sow in order to draw us back to Him.

We see God's good discipline in other books of the Bible as well. In Deuteronomy 8, for example, Moses reminded the people of their consequences in the wilderness. Then he said, "Think about it: Just as a parent disciplines a child, the Lord your God disciplines you for your own good" (v. 5). Here again we see that because God is just, He allows consequences; yet He always does it out of His great love for us. In fact, He was willing to make the ultimate sacrifice on our behalf, sending His own Son to die in our place in order to deal with our sin.

So, when we are tempted to blame God for hard or painful things in life, we need to remember the three categories of suffering and God's character, trusting His goodness even when we don't understand our circumstances. Especially then.

We all make bad choices daily. And if you are God's child, He is probably faithfully disciplining you in at least one area right now. Where do you see Him allowing consequences in your life? Is it relationships, finances, marital issues, parenting, time management, ministry, or some other area?

As God corrects us, we are wise to repent and turn to Him. Sadly, oftentimes we tend to find someone or some circumstance to blame.

Finding a Target

When I was a kid, my dad occasionally would wake everyone in the house and call us to hunt for his lost keys so that he could leave for work. The apple doesn't fall far from the tree, only with me it's my cell phone. I never remember where I left it and often blame my kids or husband for moving it. Usually I find it in my purse or jacket pocket—right where I left it. Until it is found, I am sure that someone else is to blame. It's humbling when the facts prove that my accusations are unfounded.

The people of Judah had problems with blaming as well. They often claimed they were innocent of wrongdoing and denied that they worshipped idols (Jeremiah 2:23). They did not want to take personal responsibility for playing a part in the consequences headed their way. But God didn't leave them to wonder why they were headed for judgment. In Jeremiah 17:5 we find God clearly communicating His answer to the question *Why?* The judgments of God against the people of Judah—which consisted of war, poverty, hunger, exile, and utter defeat—were the result of their own sin. God wasn't shy about being specific about H:s people's offenses.

He did not leave the people of Judah to wonder why these terrible circumstances were upon them. He was clear. If they wanted to blame someone, they needed to hold up a mirror. They shouldn't have been surprised at God's heavy hand against them. After all, He laid out instructions for them when they first entered the land seven hundred years earlier.

God didn't expected His children to read His mind about His expectations. He gave them clear instructions, spelling out both the consequences of disobedience and the blessings of obedience.

God put two choices before His people—life or death. He instructed His people, and when they got off course, He sent His prophets to repeat the message. Since sin entered the world, God's message has been the same: "Turn from your sins and turn to Me." Both John the Baptist (Luke 3:3) and Jesus (Matthew 4:17) came preaching this message.

It's easy to look at the people of Judah and think they were crazy not to follow and love God. After all, they had been given clear instructions, they had the warnings of the prophets calling them to repent, and they even had the example of their neighbors in Israel, who were reaping the consequences of their own sin. (Israel, the Northern Kingdom, had gone into captivity one hundred years before Babylon invaded Judah.) Yet in Jeremiah 3:6-10, we see God telling the people of Judah that they didn't learn from the sins of Israel. Though they had the law and the prophets, they chose not to heed the warnings and to stubbornly "eat the bitter fruit of living their own way" (Proverbs 1:31).

It's time we quit the blame game, take a good look at our own sin, and begin to walk the road of repentance. We can't change anyone else, but we can allow God to change us.

Are we so different? Who do you blame when life gets rough? Human nature calls out, "It's not my fault! If only I had a great marriage.... If only my kids behaved like so-and-so's kids.... If only I had more money.... If only my friends supported me.... If only I was appreciated at work...." What's your "if only"? Most of us have one. But no matter where we choose to place the blame, the truth is that we need to get honest about our own failures. Are we loving God, walking in His ways, and following His commands as laid out in Deuteronomy? Do our prayer lives reflect it? Do our financial choices show that God is our priority? Do we regularly serve others and share our faith? Does our heart break for the things that break God's heart? Could it be that the problem lies within us?

Let's take an inventory of what we have today:

- Clear instructions on how to live from the complete Word of God.
- Access to great preaching, teaching, and Bible studies through our local churches and Christian media.
- Examples of many who have chosen not to walk with God and are eating the bitter fruit of their choices.
- Examples of many others who are living radically for Christ.

If anything, I believe we could be held more accountable than the people of Jeremiah's day because of the opportunity we have to know and study the truth. We have God's Word in its entirety, as well as the indwelling Holy Spirit to guide us in applying it. It's time we quit the blame game, take a good look at our own sin, and begin to walk the road of repentance. We can't change anyone else, but we can allow God to change *us*.

The tendency we all have toward passing the buck is one of my least favorite topics. As frustrated as I've been with my children's overt attempts to explain away their bad choices, I know I'm also often looking for a target to blame. Just as I desire my kids to own up to their mistakes so that they can learn from them, God wants us to turn from our sin so that we can turn to Him. He wants to give us mercy, and He calls us to recognize our bad choices and repent. I'm thankful that as we evaluate our lives and seek to take whatever steps necessary to follow Him, He redeems even our mistakes to bring us into closer relationship with Him. The only thing that can keep us from His mercy is our own perilous pride.

Perilous Pride

When I was pregnant with our twins, I became really sick. As I've mentioned, I thought I was only having one baby until ten days before they were born; but the reality of double girl hormones wasn't lost on my body! I couldn't keep much food down for around twenty weeks. I can't call it morning sickness because it was more like all-day sickness. My son was three and a half at the time and very active. I am not the gal who likes to admit I can't do something, especially something like taking care of one child.

My favorite movie line is from *The Rookie*. The main character says he should stop pursuing his dream of playing baseball to come home and help his wife, and she replies, "I'm a Texas woman, which means I don't need the help of a man to keep things running."[2] I want to be like her—independent and able to take care of everything without needing the help of others. (Did I mention I'm from Texas?)

It pained me to admit I could do little more than lie in bed, moan, and try to keep down what food I could manage. I remember a friend from church I barely knew stopping by to pick up my son for the afternoon so I could rest. She always teases me now about my disheveled hair, bathrobe, and mumbled instructions about how to take care of him. Those days were humbling. I hated the feeling of being dependent on others and did a lot of moping and blaming during those dark days. While I wish I could say I drew close to the Lord during that time, in reality I did a lot of wallowing in self-pity.

The words *pride* and *proud* are mentioned in the Book of Jeremiah numerous times. Pride is an elusive thing. It can take many forms. Simply put, it is an obsession with self. Apart from God's work in our lives, every one of us will make decisions to serve our own interests—to paint ourselves in the best light and work out situations to our benefit. This is the core of our sin problem. We all battle daily against the sin of pride, and we will fight it until the day we are free from sin forever in heaven with Jesus.

Sometimes we experience a different kind of pride called "reverse pride." This is when we are so down on ourselves that others may think it's humility. We might claim we are "no good" or "not of any value." But this is self-abasement, not humility. God says that we are fearfully and wonderfully made and have great value as His children (see Psalm 139:14 and Jeremiah 1). When we put ourselves down with negative statements—"I could never be good at that"; "They won't want me to come because I never add anything to the conversation"; "My nose is too big. I'm so fat. I wish I looked like her"; "I don't think I should attempt that; I probably won't be any good at it"—this is not humility. This is still pride, which demonstrates a lack of belief in what God says about our value.

The nations surrounding Israel and Judah struggled with pride. In Jeremiah 46–51, God lays out His judgments against these foreign nations. In these chapters we see that although God has a special love for Judah, He cares about *all* people and gives them a chance to turn to Him. God has always loved and adopted those who wish to follow Him. We see that God is holy and holds every nation accountable for its own sins using the same standard. He calls these nations back to Himself in the same way that He indicted Judah in the previous chapters.

One at a time, God used the words of Jeremiah to tell the nations of Egypt, Philistia, Moab, Ammon, Daasucs, Kedar, Hazor, Elam, and Babylon that they would be judged, as found in chapters 46–51. God didn't leave them to wonder why they would be punished but specifically told them about how their idolatry, violence, and deception would bring a day of reckoning for each of them.

In Jeremiah 48:7, we find that the nation of Moab had trusted in their "wealth and skill." They deceived themselves into thinking that every good thing in their lives was their own doing. This resembles the American mind-sets of "I deserve it," "I am powerful," and "Look at all I have accomplished." Hard work, goal setting, and material goods are not inherently wrong, but we would be wise to always remember that "apart from [Him we] can do nothing" (John 15:5). Anything good we accomplish originated in God, who gave us the talent and resources. We need to remember the Moabites so that we will not become like them—trusting in wealth and skill while forgetting the God in heaven who has given these gifts.

Now let's turn to God's special people of Judah. Surely they humbled themselves in contrast to their surrounding neighbors, right? Well, not so much. They took a little too much pride in their status as God's people. They forgot that what made them special was God's love for them, not their own strength or status. In Jeremiah 5:12-13 they say, "He won't bother us! / No disasters will come upon us," and in Jeremiah 21:13 they boast, "No one can touch us here. / No one can break in here." Pride had gotten the best of them to say the least!

God takes pride very seriously because it is a huge barrier to close relationship with Him. We can't embrace God until we recognize our need for Him. No clearer does He spell it out than in these verses from Jeremiah 9:

> This is what the LORD says:
> "Don't let the wise boast in their wisdom,
> or the powerful boast in their power,
> or the rich boast in their riches.
> But those who wish to boast
> should boast in this alone:
> that they truly know me and understand that I am
> the LORD
> who demonstrates unfailing love
> and who brings justice and righteousness
> to the earth,
> and that I delight in these things.
> I, the LORD, have spoken! (vv. 23-24)

God weeps when we become self-absorbed because we are missing out on the life He designed us to live in fellowship with Him. He knows pride will lead us to emptiness, and it breaks His heart to the point of tears.

As we've seen, our sin nature has a natural bent toward pride, and none of us escapes this tendency without frequent self-evaluation and repentance. Doing regular heart and motive checks as we talked about in chapter 4 can help us see when we are wearing pride without realizing it. Even those of us who are devoted followers of God can allow pride to creep into our hearts and minds.

Another way we can keep our pride in check is to invite a good friend to hold us accountable by pointing it out from time to time. Jeremiah did this for his scribe—and possibly his only friend—who was named Baruch. (If it's hard to believe Jeremiah might have had only one friend, remember how unpopular his messages made him.) Baruch recorded the messages from the Lord and sometimes delivered them to kings for Jeremiah. In Jeremiah 45, the Lord lovingly warns Baruch through Jeremiah about the danger of going down the road of self-focus:

> "This is what the LORD, the God of Israel, says to you, Baruch: You have said, 'I am overwhelmed with trouble! Haven't I had enough pain already? And now the LORD has added more! I am worn out from sighing and can find no rest.'
>
> "Baruch, this is what the LORD says: 'I will destroy this nation that I built. I will uproot what I planted. Are you seeking great things for yourself? Don't do it! I will bring great disaster upon all these people; but I will give you your life as a reward wherever you go.'" (vv. 2-5)

Baruch's frustrations were well founded. He had truly suffered, just as Jeremiah had. They lived in a time when bread was scarce, enemies invaded regularly, and they publicly wrote and recorded messages that weren't popular. Though we often stroke and coddle our friends when they are making a case for injustice in their lives, Jeremiah was kind but bold in his response to Baruch.

The battle against selfish pride is clear in this passage. When we begin to walk along the road of self-absorption, God says to us, *"Don't do it!"*

When I become focused on myself, I notice a few things I would rather not admit:

- I tend to brag or name-drop about things God has done through me as if I deserved some of the credit.
- I fall into old sin patterns with my thought life, namely judging others.
- I find myself in conflicts—with my husband, my children, or my friends.
- I begin to see others for what they have or haven't done to support me.
- I worry about money and try to figure out how to solve issues on my own.

Did you notice some common words in these admissions? *Me. My. Myself.* Yuck. I want to pretend that it's not true and that I'm naturally humble and kind, but the reality is that apart from Jesus, my defaults smack of perilous pride.

I hope you can think of at least one of your selfish tendencies, because my list took me all of thirty seconds to write, and I could go on! Pride is dangerous. If we don't deal with it, we must brace ourselves for a fall. This is true for us not only on a corporate level as a nation but also on a personal level as individuals. Recognizing our pride and addressing it with God through prayer is critical if we are to going to quit playing the blame game. And this requires more than just "going through the motions."

Whatever they might be, religious practices become empty when our motivation is anything other than our devoted love for God.

Going Through the Motions

This morning I found myself at my aerobics class lost in a reverie of thought. My body was still mimicking the teacher's movements but definitely lacked the sharpness of intentionality in the moves. I wasn't stretching my arms as far as I could or lifting my knees high. I wasn't focused on what I was doing because my mind was drifting from an item I needed to add to my grocery list to the words I needed to respond to an uncomfortable text I had received that morning. Is anyone with me in struggling to focus? A similar thing can happen in our relationship with God. If we're not careful, the practice of religious rituals or habits such as prayer, worship, Bible study, and Holy Communion can lose meaning for us, leaving us feeling that they somehow "appease" God or fulfill some kind of duty or obligation. Whatever they might be, religious practices become empty when our motivation is anything other than our devoted love for God. It's like when a husband and wife start going through the motions rather than demonstrating genuine love for each other. Who wants a spouse whose mind is always somewhere else and whose actions are perfunctory? Who wants to be given a kiss out of duty or obligation?

That's exactly what had happened to the people of Judah's worship: they were going through the motions. The priests were offering sacrifices, and false prophets were delivering messages they said were from the Lord, but their hearts were not right (see Jeremiah 23:11). Not only were they going through the motions but they also allowed their religious practices to be corrupted by pagan influences.

The people felt justified or "right with God" because they had the Temple, which they believed always would be protected by God. As one source explains, "Many Jews thought that if they were in the house of God then they would be under God's protection, and as a result [they] tended to be careless in their daily living."[3] They also expanded their religious practices as a sort of backup plan. Just in case God wasn't strong enough to save them, they would sacrifice their sons and daughters to pagan gods who might be able to help them. Though shocking and unthinkable to us, this was the result of falling in with the customary practices of their neighbors. Essentially they would do anything to try to persuade any god who might listen to help them. Even though they had little money, they would waste drink offerings to pour out to a foreign god referred to as the Queen of Heaven or buy little handmade statues in the town square that were carved in the images of other gods. But all of these practices were empty.

As we read in Jeremiah 9:25-26, God was not pleased with their empty practice of circumcision. Circumcision, which was instituted by God during the days of Abraham to set the Israelites apart, was a symbol meant to remind the people of their covenant with God (see Genesis 17:9-14). The people kept the practice but forgot the spiritual significance behind the ritual. Even here in the Old Testament God is talking about a circumcision of the heart. As we read in Romans 2:29, true circumcision is "a change of heart produced by the Spirit."

Essentially, the Judean people's practices had become empty, losing or even contradicting God's intent. The people attempted to go through the motions, and then they added horrific rituals from pagan religions, which only added to their shame. Perhaps they tried to justify this by explaining themselves, calling God unfair, or spinning the details so that others would sympathize with them. The logic might have gone something like this:

> We've done everything God said. We've given our sacrifices, circumcised our sons, visited the Temple, and tried to keep the Sabbath when nothing else was going on. Well, we've done almost everything, I guess. I mean, nobody's perfect. We have given some offerings to Baal and the Queen of Heaven, and we might have burned our children in sacrifice to these gods; but if the Lord doesn't think they're real gods, then what does it matter to Him? As long as we give Him our offerings, why should He care what we do on the side?

Now, before we judge the people of Judah, we must ask ourselves if we've ever gone through the motions or made our own determinations about what God should or shouldn't care about. I know I have. But we cannot blame Him for our partial obedience, our half-hearted attempts at following Him, and our blatant disobedience because we do not worship a god we create according to what makes sense to our mind, will, and emotions. The God we worship is the sovereign God of the Bible, the Creator of the universe, the Lord of Heaven's Armies! God is who He says He is in His Word. This is why we must read and study the Bible curiously and carefully, seeking to know the true God. Knowing God—*really* knowing Him—gives us the passion to keep our devotional time, church attendance, and ministry involvement from becoming rote, empty expressions.

Sometimes we assume that God owes us a pain-free life because we have done "our part." We went to church services twice last month and even dropped a twenty-dollar-bill in the offering plate. We made sure our kids took the right church classes, said the right spiritual words, and jumped through all the religious hoops. Then when something bad happens, we are tempted to blame God since we have paid our dues. But it doesn't work that way.

While you might nod your head, agreeing that this is wrong thinking, these thoughts can infiltrate our minds at times. I talked with a mom whose husband had just lost his job, and at the end of the conversation she made an offhanded comment, saying that God had better come through for them because they had come through for Him all their lives. I'm sure she didn't mean God owed her something—or did she? When things go wrong in my own life, I can find the same line of thinking infecting the way I process my trials. None of us is immune to finding ourselves blaming God, especially when we are in pain.

Spiritual rhythms or disciplines can be great connecting points with God in our lives. Going to church, spending time in prayer, and reading God's Word lead us into deeper relationship with Him. The danger comes when our religious practices become rote and stale. So we must constantly seek to find the meaning in our routines to keep them fresh. If we'll ask Him, God will show us specific ways we can infuse new life into any empty or lifeless spiritual habit, because He wants our connection with Him to be strong and vibrant!

Rescue Comes with Repentance

We've considered some of the pitfalls of the blame game as well as things we can do to quit this destructive game, and by now we're all well aware of the need to do just that. But awareness and action are two different things. We can desire to stop a harmful habit and even cry out to God for help, but without actions to back up our words, they are empty. When it comes to quitting the blame game, rescue comes with repentance.

Two important people in my life struggle with anger. Both love God passionately and care about their families. Both have offered apologies and expressed regret repeatedly for outbursts they wish they could take back. I believe this has contributed to my lack of enthusiasm about apologies. I reached the point when I didn't want another apology; I simply wanted the outbursts to stop. I wanted to feel peaceful instead of anxious, anticipating when their anger might erupt again. Both of these people have come a long way in their battle with anger, but I cannot say the scar of empty words hasn't stayed with me.

Words are important. According to Proverbs 18:21, they have the power of life and death. However, words of intent without follow-through are just wishful thinking. They are the New Year's resolutions we make without a plan to see them through. They are the apologies we offer even when it's obvious we don't mean it. They are the promises we make to God but don't keep (such as saying that we love God but refusing to get along with His children). They are empty words with no actions to back them up.

The people of Judah had a lot of experience in offering empty words. They cried out to God on several occasions, declaring their intent to change their ways, but there were no actions to back up their words. They didn't demonstrate true repentance.

Jeremiah spoke often about repentance. One source notes that "the Hebrew word most often used by Jeremiah for repentance is *sub*, usually translated 'return' or 'turn.' It is a key word in Jeremiah, who interpreted repentance as a reorientation of one's life...a turning away from sin and a simultaneous turning to God."[4]

Have you ever been driving the wrong way and your smart phone or GPS said, "Recalculating"? Then it rerouted you so that you were turned back toward your destination rather than away from it. A similar concept happens in life when we get off course spiritually. Once we acknowledge we are moving in the wrong direction, we must turn around—repent—and go God's new way, which gets us to the destination of intimacy with Him.

In Jeremiah 14 we see that the people of Judah were crying out for rescue, but God knew their hearts. Their motives weren't right. Listen to their cry for help and the Lord's response:

> O Hope of Israel, our Savior in times of trouble,
> why are you like a stranger to us?
> Why are you like a traveler passing through the land,
> stopping only for the night?
> Are you also confused?
> Is our champion helpless to save us?
> You are right here among us, LORD.
> We are known as your people.
> Please don't abandon us now!"
>
> So this is what the LORD says to his people:
> "You love to wander far from me
> and do not restrain yourselves.
> Therefore, I will no longer accept you as my people.
> Now I will remember all your wickedness
> and will punish you for your sins." (vv. 8-10)

They wanted God's hand of help without any relationship or repentance. It's like the rebellious teenager who consistently makes bad choices but then wants to be bailed out of the penalties every time. Softening the pain of consequences won't help the teen to change. Like a good parent, God chose to allow Judah to experience the difficulty brought upon them by their bad decisions.

There is always a penalty for sin. God is holy, and sin separates us from Him. This helps us understand why the cross is so significant. God continually offers us hope, and this hope centers on Jeremiah's prediction of a future Messiah. Although Jeremiah did not know Jesus's name, His faith in the future Savior assured his salvation as much as my faith in Jesus does. Jesus's sacrifice on the cross was the necessary payment for our sin so that we can be restored to a right relationship with God. This is the good news of the gospel. However, the gospel message also includes repentance.

Repentance is not just *admitting* our sin; it is *turning* from it. God wants more than words. Real faith reveals itself through actions. It turns away from sin and toward a holy God. Let us learn from the people of Judah that God wants us to fully yield our words and our lives to Him. When our mouths say one thing but our actions reveal something else, we are only lying to ourselves.

The people of Jeremiah's day cried out for rescue without a spirit of honesty and repentance. They cried out for help but still continued in their sinful practices. Jeremiah 5 tells about their lust, lies, and treachery. But the main issue God brings out is their lies. When pride and selfishness are ruling our lives, we tell lies about ourselves that, in effect, cause us to tell lies about God. This is what leads us down the path to blaming God for the consequences of our bad decisions.

In *Till We Have Faces* by C. S. Lewis, a girl named Orual finds that she can't see God for who He is until she understands her own pride and sin. I know this has been true for me. Here are some of the lies I sometimes tell about myself that cause me to tell lies about God:

Lies About Myself	Lies About God	Truth
I deserve better.	God hasn't provided enough.	Philippians 4:19
I'm not qualified to do that.	God's isn't able to do it through me.	Jeremiah 1
I don't need anybody.	God wants me to be independent.	Hebrews 10:24-25
My motives are right.	God says my heart is good.	Jeremiah 17:9
This is too little for God.	God doesn't care about details.	Psalm 37:23
This is too big for God.	My situation is too hard for God.	Jeremiah 32:17
My way is best.	I know better than God.	Jeremiah 6:16

These are just a few of the many distorted views that cause us to see God as unfair, unwilling, or unjust. In order to break free from these lies and the trap of wanting rescue without repentance, we must recognize our flawed thinking and then apply God's Word of truth.

Crisis prayers often fall into the category of wanting rescue without repentance. "God, help me pass this test, and I'll be really good this week." "God, if you will just make my child better, we'll go to church more." "God, change my husband, and then I'll be a better wife." These are cries for rescue.

We all need rescuing, don't we? We may not have an army invading, but I haven't met many people with problem-free lives! We ask for help with difficult relationships, work issues, marriage and/or parenting challenges, draining people, financial crises, and endless daily tasks. It's no wonder we are looking for some reprieve. God longs for us to cry out to Him; and when our struggles are a result of disobedience, He calls us to turn from our sin—repent—and walk in obedience to Him. God is always faithful to redirect us, rescuing us from a road of dangerous pitfalls. When we take personal responsibility and stop playing the blame game, we find hope in our relationship with our loving God and personal transformation as God grows our character in the process.

Dare to Hope Challenge

What are you crying out to God to rescue you from right now? Perhaps there are some action steps of repentance that God is calling you to take that relate to your rescue. For example, you might need to make an attitude adjustment in a relationship. Or maybe there are nutrition, exercise, or sleep habits that need changing for your health, or prayer and Bible study habits that require attention for your spiritual well-being. Perhaps there are spending or saving habits you need to make to improve your finances. Or it could be that you need to offer a sacrifice of your time or provide more consistent discipline with your children. Listen to God now and be open to what He says. Then put it into practice! Don't let your pride keep you from being honest with God, repenting of your sin, and experiencing the joy of rescue.

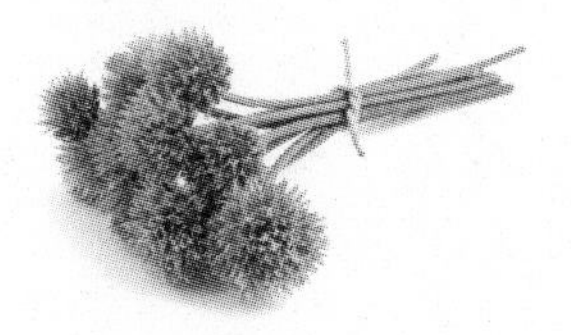

CHAPTER 6

Finding the Source of Our Hope

Pursue Intimacy with God

"For I know the plans I have for you," says the Lord. "They are plans for good and not for disaster, to give you a future and a hope."

—Jeremiah 29:11

What will they think of me? Do I fit in? Am I dressed appropriately? Does my coworker or friend think my advice is good? Are my words what they want to hear? If I'm too harsh with decision making/discipline, they will think I'm mean. If I'm too soft, they will think I'm a pushover.

Have you ever had thoughts like these? Me too.

So often we spend too much time worrying about what the spectators of our lives think of us rather than focusing on what God thinks of us. This kind of self-talk reveals that we're more concerned about what others think than we are about following the Holy Spirit's lead. We all find ourselves here when we follow the path of fearing people more than God.

In order to find the source of our hope—the source of the *daring* hope that we need in an uncertain world—we need to worry less about what others think and give our mental energy to following God. If we fear people more than God in the little things of life, such as what others think of our decision making or parenting, how will we tackle the real obstacles that threaten to take us down? When it comes to handling the uncertainties of life such as illness, relationship breakdowns, political turmoil, economic downturns, and job loss, finding and focusing on the source of our hope is critical. Let's explore what this looks like to get a picture of what it means to have intimacy with Jesus.

An Audience of One

Finding the source of our hope means living for an audience of One. Striving to please God alone will get us through anything we might face in life. Jeremiah has much to teach us about this.

God had led His people faithfully, but they continued to seek other false gods. Speaking through the prophet Jeremiah, God described what their chosen path away from Him would be like:

> "Your wickedness will punish you;
> your backsliding will rebuke you.
> Consider then and realize
> how evil and bitter it is for you
> when you forsake the LORD your God
> and have no awe of me,"
> declares the LORD, the LORD Almighty.
> (Jeremiah 2:19 NIV)

Did the words *evil* and *bitter* jump out at you? I don't know about you, but those two words don't top the list of my goals in life. Many translations use these two words because the meanings of the Hebrew words are so clear. The word used for evil is *ra'*, which means evil, very bad, or wicked;[1] and the word used for bitter is *mar*,[2] which is the root of the name Naomi gave herself after the death of her husband and sons (Ruth 1:20). We never desire for these words to be associated with our lives, yet this is how God describes the consequences of not fearing Him.

When we live like Jeremiah,
putting fear of God over fear of
people or circumstances,
the road is not problem-free,
but it is blessed.

The people of Judah trusted in political alliances with other nations even though God wanted to lead them. We do a similar thing today when we look to things other than God—such as 401(k)s, drugs or alcohol, or social media, to name a few. We may not be facing a Babylonian army, but we do have real fears about what could happen in the future. When challenges such as health issues, work problems or job loss, relational strains, financial worries, rebellious children, marital tension, and betrayal threaten to overpower us, where do we turn? Do we say we trust God with our mouths while our actions reveal otherwise?

The antidote for the fear of people and circumstances is the fear of God. This isn't the kind of fear that makes you want to hide in a closet from an abusive parent; it's a holy fear. One writer explains it this way: "Such awe attracts you to God; it does not repel or leave you feeling shame. It makes you want to come to him and know him. When the fear of the Lord matures in you, Christ becomes irresistible."[3] As we come to know God more—His power, love, and ways—we begin to trust Him more with our fears. People and circumstances that used to scare us and keep us up at night lose their hold over us in light of our relationship with the Lord of Heaven's Armies. And as we follow Him closely, walking in obedience and trusting Him with our lives, we discover that we have nothing to fear.

Whether it is little insecurities about what others think about us or big decisions that tempt us to trust in things we can see and control rather than in God, fearing people and circumstances will always get us into big trouble and take us places we don't want to go. Living to please the spectators on the road of faith leads to manipulation, worry, and disappointment—and ultimately to discipline from a loving Father who wants to lead us back to Him as our source of hope.

We need to evaluate what is bigger in our lives: people and circumstances, or God? When we live like Jeremiah, putting fear of God over fear of people or circumstances, the road is not problem-free, but it is *blessed*.

This topic hits home for me. I used to ride the approval roller coaster. Now, I like roller coasters, but this one is not fun! When others praised and complimented me, my children, or my ministry, I soared. However, when people were critical of anything from my haircut to my husband, I spiraled downward into defeat and shame. Over a period of time, through a gradual process of naming this issue, getting at the root of its pull on my heart, and devouring God's Word, God freed me from my approval addiction. I now can say with the apostle Paul, "If I were still trying to please people, I would not be a servant of Christ" (Galatians 1:10c NIV). By teaching me to look for approval in the eyes of Him alone, God has blessed and freed my relationships with others. Though I must continually surrender this area of my life to Christ, today I am free to truly love those around me no matter if they throw me flowers or stones.

When those stones come flying at you, as they inevitably will, remember there is one Spectator who is crazy about you. His name is Jesus, and He wants you to follow His path because He adores you and knows the dangers of the approval roller coaster. And what's more, He has *good* plans ahead for you.

Good Plans Ahead

Finding the source of our hope means believing with confidence that God has good plans in store for us—even when life takes an unexpected or tragic turn.

The movie *Soul Surfer* is about teen surfer Bethany Hamilton, who was attacked by a shark and lost her arm. In one scene of the movie, Bethany is attending a church youth group meeting where the youth leader shows them a couple of magnified images and asks them to guess what each object is. They come up with some funny answers. After showing each magnified image, the youth leader shows a photo that reveals the full object. The point she makes is that it can be hard to make sense of things when you're looking at them really closely; the same thing, she says, is true in life. Sometimes we need a different perspective. We tend to live life "close up" without taking the time to back up and see what our circumstances look like from a year out, five years out, or in light of eternity.

If we take a full view of what is perhaps the most-quoted verse from the Book of Jeremiah, we can learn something about perspective: "'For I know the plans I have for you,' says the LORD. 'They are plans for good and not for disaster, to give you a future and a hope'" (29:11).

Now, I don't want to burst the bubble of hope that this verse gives us, but we need to be careful not to overlook all that is going on here. If we go back and look at verse 10, God says His people will remain in Babylon for seventy years and then God will do all those good things He promised.

We like to think that this feel-good verse means God is going to change our circumstances right now. God is our hope, and He *does* have good plans for our future. However, for the people of Judah that hope included seventy more years of exile before circumstances changed. Often it is our perspective that needs to change in order for us to see the good plans and the hope that God has for us now.

Bethany Hamilton lost her arm in a shark attack, and that wasn't going to change. But she chose to get a new perspective on her difficult circumstance and see how God could use it. She put her trust in God, pursuing Him through her many trials, and she discovered that He was faithful and had good plans for her as a surfer even after a shark attack left her with only one arm.

Jeremiah 29:11 is not a promise to restore lost limbs or broken relationships, fill bank accounts, or make life problem-free. It is a promise to love and bless us even when times are tough.

Daniel was one of the people of Judah carried off in the early Babylonian invasion. He probably heard Jeremiah speak messages from God. Daniel set his mind to follow God faithfully, even when others were conforming to Babylonian culture. Though Daniel remained in exile with his people in Babylon, God protected and blessed him throughout those years of captivity.

Before they were taken captive, the people of Judah faced many other difficulties during the time of Jeremiah's prophecies. They suffered financial strain because they had to pay tribute to other nations, they endured corrupt leaders, and they lived in fear of Babylon—fears they saw come to pass. All of these difficulties left the people feeling desperate and unstable. At times I'm sure they found it difficult to believe that God's plans for them could be good in the midst of all these struggles.

Jeremiah 29:11 is just one of many verses in Jeremiah's book that reveals God's heart to bring blessing even in difficult circumstances. There are many other passages that reveal God's heart to bless His people with good plans. (Check out Jeremiah 30:7-11, 18-22; 31:1-14; and 50:4-7.)

God wants to bless us—to give us rest, hope, and peace. And these are good plans! However, because God knows that we cannot have these things apart from Him and that we are prone to wander, sometimes He allows difficult circumstances so that we will come back to Him. As C. S. Lewis wrote, "God whispers to us in our pleasures, speaks in our conscience, but shouts in our pain: it is His megaphone to rouse a deaf world."[4] Pain tends to get our attention when we stray, doesn't it?

Our good God delights in providing for us, but as we saw in the preceding chapter, He will not enable us in our sin and disobedience. As a parent, I have a fuller understanding of this aspect of God's love. I want to spoil my children with every good thing in my power to give them; but when I see them feeling or acting entitled, ungrateful, unhealthy, and ultimately miserable in their selfishness, I know that too much of a good thing has been detrimental. In those moments when their pain comes as a result of their own selfish choices, I still comfort them just as I do at other times, but I also allow natural and logical consequences to have their full effect so that my children can be motivated to refrain from repeating the same mistakes.

God knows and understands our human state. He knows our bent toward sin. That's why He sent Jesus as a sacrifice, prophesying about Him through Jeremiah so many years before His coming. Ultimately, God's best plan for all who follow Him is spending eternity with Him. While in this life there is much suffering, in the next there will be no tears. Even if the world crumbles around us or we must face many years in a difficult circumstance, we can know with confidence that God's plans are good because one day we will see Him face-to-face. Talk about a future and a hope!

To guard against those times when life seems devoid of hope and we lose sight of God's good plans, we need to meditate on Scripture and begin to hide the words in our hearts. When we meditate on the promises of God, it teaches us to lean into the Source of our hope—who longs for relationship with us and always offers us a way back home.

God Brings Us Back

Finding the source of our hope means trusting that there's always a way back to right relationship with God.

In the Book of Jeremiah, we find God's repeated declarations of intent to exile His people from their land because of their habitual, unrepentant sin. As we've explored, sin separates us from God, driving a wedge into the close relationship He desires to have with us. Now let's examine more closely God's heart that always longs to draw us back.

To get a fuller understanding of God's hopeful plan against a backdrop of idolatry, disobedience, and hard hearts, let's journey from the days of Jeremiah back to the days of the United Kingdom in Israel. Bear with me for this brief history review; I promise it has significant implications for our understanding of God's longing to draw us back to Him.

Kings first began ruling Israel in 1050 BC when the people begged God for a king so that they could be like other nations. This was roughly five hundred years before Jeremiah's proclamations from God. God warned the people against wanting a monarchy, but He gave them Saul as their first king after their constant pestering. (Our God doesn't force His way on us. Sometimes He lets us learn through experience that His way is best.)

After Saul, David became king and ruled as "a man after [God's] own heart" (1 Samuel 13:14). During David's reign, we see a clear picture of God's desire to look for ways to bring us back to Him when we have been disobedient. In 2 Samuel 14:14, we find these words: "But

God does not just sweep life away; instead, he devises ways to bring us back when we have been separated from him." After David's death, his son Solomon became king and built the Temple. In Solomon's prayer of dedication of the Temple found in 1 Kings 8, we find a reference to the days of Jeremiah that reveals God's desire to draw His people back.

King Solomon's son Rehoboam inherited only the lands of Judah and Benjamin, and the other ten tribes of Israel split off under Jeroboam's leadership to form the nation of Israel. So Judah and Israel became two separate nations that often fought each other. Israel abandoned their God, and God sent many prophets with His messages of repentance (such as, Elijah, Elisha, Hosea, and Amos). Once again we see God's heart to draw His people back. Finally, after their refusal to repent, the people of Israel were carried off into captivity by Assyria in 722 BC.

Unfortunately, the people of Judah did not learn from Israel's punishment. They had a few godly kings who led some revivals, but by Jeremiah's day, wickedness and sin had a foothold in the people's heart. At that time God sent Jeremiah to call them to repentance—yet again demonstrating His longing to draw His people back.

Over and over there is a pattern of hope in the history of God and His people. It looks something like this:

> God knows our tendency to sin.
> He gives us an opportunity to repent.
> He forgives us and restores us when we turn to Him.

Even here in the Old Testament we see the beauty of God's gospel! We resemble the people of Jeremiah's day more than we care to admit. We worship counterfeits, struggle with a lack of listening, suffer from hard-heartedness, and often blame others when we mess up. First Kings 8:46 says, "And who has never sinned?" We all struggle daily with the "sin disease" that wants to kill our soul. Yet our God longs for us to return to Him and offers us a way back. He says we are to confess, repent, and find forgiveness.

Unfortunately, the people of Jeremiah's day wouldn't listen. So in 586 BC, Babylon invaded and destroyed Jerusalem. It may seem pretty bleak for God's people at this point. After all, where is the hope in exile, destruction, and punishment?

Actually, we can see God's longing for His people even in the midst of the promised punishment for sin. You see, God offers hope for a remnant who are willing to follow Him—and this remnant is not a leftover piece of fabric! The *Holman Bible Dictionary* defines a remnant as "something left over, especially the righteous people of God after divine judgment."[5]

The concept of "remnant" is found throughout the pages of Scripture, reminding us that even in times of God's judgment, He offers hope to any who will return to Him. We see Noah's family left as a remnant after the flood. When Elijah claims to be the only follower of God left, God reminds him that a remnant of seven thousand remain faithful (1 Kings 19:10-18). Jeremiah also predicts a future day when God will bring His people back to their promised land.

God often speaks of the remnant of His people with words of hope and compassion. They have been through a lot of difficulty, which has left them humble and ready to obey. These are the people who have learned to trust in Him through their struggles. Here we see God gathering His people with promises of rest, peace, and forgiveness.

Not everyone, however, chooses to practice humility and trust in God during tough times. So we find another remnant in Jeremiah that did not learn the lesson of repentance after the catastrophe of exile (see Jeremiah 42:18-20; 44:12-14; and 47:4-5). God will use anything to bring us near to Him, but He will not force our hand. Although the remnant mentioned in Scripture is usually connected with repentance and hope, there is another remnant made up of those who endure the Lord's discipline and still insist on going their own way. Because of the hardness of their hearts and their refusal to turn to God, the plans God has for this unrepentant remnant are more discipline, not peace. This makes me want to learn my lessons quickly so that I can get to the hopeful part! How about you? Because God loves us and knows what is best for us, He calls us to turn back to Him, give up control, and follow Him wholeheartedly.

Once we turn back to God, He asks us to be *daring* with hope. Sometimes that means being a remnant of only one. Jeremiah certainly knew what that felt like! Yet God reassured him that he could stand alone—that God would rescue and protect him. Like Jeremiah, even when we must stand alone as the only one in our family, our friend group, or even our church who dares to hope in God in tough times, God promises to be our Protector. We can trust God, even when we don't "feel" that we can.

For you and me, standing alone doesn't usually mean preaching a message of surrender as it did for Jeremiah. When I think back on times when I had to stand alone, I recall being teased in high school because I chose to be morally pure. Through the years I have been blessed to have friends in the body of Christ who have stood with me at different times for different reasons; however, there have been a few very lonely times when even close friends couldn't understand some of my decisions. It has been those times, through many tears and heartbreak, that a sweet closeness with Christ has sustained me even when I felt alone.

I've read the stories of many missionaries, and I've found that the real movers and shakers for God—servants such as Gladys Aylward, Hudson Taylor, George Mueller—faced many people who questioned their desire to follow Christ in the ways that they did. They had to stand alone. They were discouraged, misunderstood, and laughed at—not only by the world but also by people in the church—for doing daring things in obedience to Christ. Though none of them had to bury underwear, hang out in a muddy cistern, or wear a wooden yoke in the streets as Jeremiah did, they each had to take bold stands in the name of Christ.

Though we must always be sure that what we feel called to do is a leading of the Holy Spirit, we must be obedient to a call we are certain is from God even if others believe it is crazy, dangerous, or radical. We must be willing to stand alone for God, trusting He will protect and sustain us.

Whether we're a remnant of one or many, the hopeful message of the remnant is that God softens and teaches us through every trial or challenge so that we will know Him in a more intimate way. He is always devising ways to bring us back to Him or draw us even closer. Even in those times when we choose to go our own way, He gives us opportunities to recognize our sin so that we may turn from it and toward our God. He is *always* ready to forgive and restore our relationship. There is no situation or sin problem that is hopeless.

Let me say that again: *There is no situation or sin problem that is hopeless!* Let those words sink deep into your heart and mind. The God of hope longs for you to walk closely with Him. In fact, He desires it so much that he sent His Son, the promised Messiah, to set things right at last.

The Promised Messiah

Finding the source of our hope means trusting in what has been accomplished through the death and resurrection of Jesus Christ, the promised Messiah. Even if you are familiar with the gospel story and the work of the cross, I invite you to lean in with fresh ears and hear anew what Christ has done for you—because it is our greatest and ultimate hope!

Six hundred years before Mary would be visited by an angel, God promised us a Messiah through the prophet Jeremiah. And just as he repeated phrases of importance throughout his book to get the people's attention—such as the description of the people's abandonment of God as the fountain of living water (Jeremiah 2:13 and 17:13), among others—it's no surprise that God would have him repeat truths about the the coming Messiah for emphasis.

Both Jeremiah 23:5-8 and 33:14-18 describe the One who is coming to save God's people in the future. The name used for God in both of these passages is "The Lord Is Our Righteousness," Jehovah Tsidkenu.[6] We see again and again in the Book of Jeremiah that we can't have righteousness on our own. So in these verses God was forthtelling the future in which He would send a Messiah to be righteousness for us.

The New Testament sheds further light on what Jeremiah's words promised:

> For the sin of this one man, Adam, caused death to rule over many. But even greater is God's

> wonderful grace and his gift of righteousness, for all who receive it will live in triumph over sin and death through this one man, Jesus Christ.
>
> Yes, Adam's one sin brings condemnation for everyone, but Christ's one act of righteousness brings a right relationship with God and new life for everyone. (Romans 5:17-18)

> For they don't understand God's way of making people right with himself. Refusing to accept God's way, they cling to their own way of getting right with God by trying to keep the law. For Christ has already accomplished the purpose for which the law was given. As a result, all who believe in him are made right with God. (Romans 10:3-4)

> So we are Christ's ambassadors; God is making his appeal through us. We speak for Christ when we plead, "Come back to God!" For God made Christ, who never sinned, to be the offering for our sin, so that we could be made right with God through Christ. (2 Corinthians 5:20-21)

Did you catch it? God makes us right with Him through Christ. Even as Jeremiah prophesied, God knew that He would send Christ to be our righteousness. He knew our need for a Savior, and He offered hope to the remnant that the Messiah would one day come. How awesome for *us* that we know that Jesus has already come and paid the penalty for our sin! Our constant bent toward foolishness and our desperately wicked hearts (Jeremiah 17:9) are constant reminders of our need to depend on Him. Thankfully, His righteousness is part of the armor of God given to protect our hearts.

According to Ephesians 6:14, God's righteousness is the breastplate. Yes, His righteousness is the breastplate that protects us from thinking we can be righteous on our own. I don't think it's a coincidence that righteousness is what God gave us to protect our hearts. We all battle guilt, fear, and condemnation from the enemy, who tempts us to sin and then throws our failure in our faces—such as when we are tempted to compromise. Whether we are debating to skip our prayer time, tell a lie, or violate our conscience in some way, the words of the enemy say, "Do it, nothing will happen." Then when we give in to that temptation, the accuser comes right back at us with shame saying, "Look what you did! You are a bad person." But when we inevitably fall prey and mess up, God calls us to turn to Him in repentance rather than run from Him in shame. When we understand that He sent Christ to be our righteousness so that we can be made right with Him regardless of our screwups, it protects our hearts from shame. I wonder if you can relate to needing righteousness to protect your heart? These are truths I must come back to continually as I remember the power of grace so that I don't allow the enemy's voice to have the final say.

I invite you to join me in putting on the breastplate of righteousness *right now* through prayer, praising God that He sent Jesus to be your righteousness to free you from guilt and shame:

> God, thank You for the armor You have provided.
> You know these battles I am fighting. Place the
> breastplate of your righteousness over my heart
> right now. Help me to walk in the freedom You

purchased for me on the cross. Let the enemy's attempts to attack me with shame and guilt bounce right off Your strong armor that protects my heart. Amen.

Jeremiah not only taught about Christ coming to be our righteousness but also spoke clearly about the new covenant that would come to make the way for us to be right with God. Jeremiah 31:31-37 gives a snapshot of a day in the future when there would be a new covenant, and the Ten Commandments would be more than just laws written in stone:

> It is the LORD who provides the sun to light the day
> and the moon and stars to light the night,
> and who stirs the sea into roaring waves.
> His name is the LORD of Heaven's Armies,
> and this is what he says:
> "I am as likely to reject my people Israel
> as I am to abolish the laws of nature!"
> This is what the LORD says:
> "Just as the heavens cannot be measured
> and the foundations of the earth cannot
> be explored,
> so I will not consider casting them away
> for the evil they have done.
> I, the LORD, have spoken!
>
> (Jeremiah 31:35-37)

God says that He is as likely to break the new covenant as He is to do away with the laws of nature. What an amazing thought! God will do away with gravity before He will abandon us!

In the Old Testament, people were saved by faith in the coming Messiah. They didn't know His name or exactly how the prophecies would be fulfilled, but it was their faith in the Messiah that made them right with God. The Temple sacrifices, priesthood, and even the Temple itself were all a foretaste of what would be fulfilled in Christ. In the New Testament we see Christ identified as our High Priest (Hebrews 4:14) as well as the final sacrifice for sin (Hebrews 10:1-10). In Hebrews 10:9 we read this about Christ: "Then he said, 'Look, I have come to do your will.' He cancels the first covenant in order to put the second into effect."

All of this shows us that God gave those living under the old covenant (Old Testament) glimpses ahead to the Messiah in whom they were placing their faith and hope. They didn't know about the cross or the nails or the crown of thorns, and they did not fully understand how this Messiah would rescue them; but they knew they needed saving.

If we were to draw a picture to represent salvation for those living before and after the cross, it would look something like this:

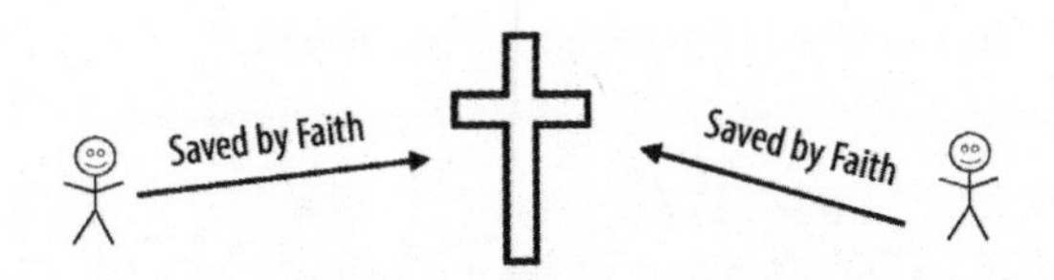

The Lord tells us that He is the true hope of Israel (Jeremiah 17:13). Jesus is the ultimate fulfillment of that hope. He came to give us life, to be our righteousness, to be the bridge from sinful humanity to a holy God.

Though our sin separates us from God, He longs to be close to us.

He wants us to know Him. So He sent Christ, His Son, as the perfect sacrifice to take the payment for all our sins upon Himself. He made a new covenant so that when we accept Christ's payment on the cross by faith, we can have a relationship with a holy God. Now when God the Father looks down on us, He sees us through the lens of Christ's sacrifice. He sees us as righteous because of what Christ has done for us. This frees us from our shame, our guilt, and our fear. Oh, what a Savior!

I understood this for the first time as a nine-year-old girl. I remember watching my brother and sister fighting on the porch through the screen door, thinking, "They have already decided to follow Christ." I purposed in my heart that I would not decide to follow Christ until I could be good all the time. I knew I wasn't ready. Then a few months later in Sunday school, a sweet teacher explained to me that I didn't have to clean myself up for God. I just had to come to Him and recognize my sin because I would never get rid of it on my own. For the first time I understood that I didn't have to be "good enough" for God; I only needed to accept His payment for my sin on the cross so that He could become "The Lord Is My Righteousness." This began my journey of walking with Christ.

At times I still struggle with seeking approval from God based on my performance. Because we live in a performance-based culture, most of us share this struggle from time to time. When we're doing well in obeying God, a tendency for pride creeps in, and when we fail, shame often comes knocking at our door. So when we sense we are heading down this path of performance-based acceptance, we can stop and remind ourselves of God's grace through Christ.

I like what Philip Yancey has written about grace: "Grace means there is nothing I can do to make God love me more, and nothing I can do to make God love me less. It means that I, even I who deserve the opposite, am invited to take my place at the table in God's family."[7] Wow! Think about that. Christ's sacrifice made it possible for each of us to be at the table as part of God's family. And *nothing* we've done or could ever do can separate us from God's love. (Do I hear a hallelujah?)

Jeremiah looked forward to this new covenant with anticipation. We look backward to Christ's finished work on the cross with gratefulness. Through faith in the revelation God has provided, we trust Him to be our righteousness and give us *all* the riches of God's kingdom.

Full Access

Finding the source of our hope means having *full access* to the riches of God's kingdom. I love some of the things that give me full access when I buy a membership to them. Amazon Prime means I have full access to free two-day shipping! Netflix gives me full access to all the shows included in their service.

While following God isn't a membership club, full access for us as believers means we not only have a seat at God's table but also have inherited all the benefits of His kingdom. And we're not just talking about heaven here; the riches of His kingdom are for us here and now through Christ. Talk about hope in an uncertain world!

Through the prophet Jeremiah, God spoke of a day of restoration that was coming, reassuring the people that His discipline wouldn't last forever. It never does. In fact, He uses every bit of it to bring about a singleness of heart and mind that realizes He alone is worthy of our complete trust. He alone is the Source of our hope.

Eleven power-packed words of Jeremiah 32:38 define this hope, which is our everlasting covenant with God: *They will be my people, and I will be their God.* Our hope rests in this statement. No matter the outcome of any election, the heights and depths of our economics, or the opinions of others, each of us can belong to God. In an unstable world, He will always be our God.

In the next verses, God goes on to make even more promises to those who choose to follow Him. Jesus fulfills all of these promises. He ushered in the everlasting covenant through His sacrifice. He made the way for us to be God's people through His shed blood on the cross. Then He rose again to new life, offering us resurrection power to help us live victoriously. He even finds "joy [in] doing good" for us (32:41). He longs for us to put our hope in Him so that we can have a close relationship with Him.

Part of this new everlasting covenant that Jeremiah foretold concerns our direct access to God. We read about the priests and the sacrifices they offered in the Temple throughout Jeremiah's prophecy. Then in chapter 33, Jeremiah speaks about a line of kings and priests that will come from David's descendants.

The author of the New Testament Book of Hebrews knew these prophecies of Jeremiah well. In Hebrews 10:8-18, we get a clear picture of how Christ fulfills Jeremiah's prophecy. The writer even quotes directly from Jeremiah's book. This new covenant through Christ is full access to eternal life with God and abundant life starting right now!

Think about this: If you could have access to a great Christian leader in our day, who would it be? Now imagine if that person gave you his or her personal phone number and said, "Call or text me anytime you have questions or are struggling. I will pray for you, counsel you, and encourage you." Would you lose the number and never contact the person, or would you call often to build a relationship?

The question facing us is this: Are we taking full advantage of our full access to the One who is our source of hope? Others can help us, but that doesn't even compare to what God offers us through a relationship with Him. Although sin separates us from God, Christ restores our relationship through His sacrifice on the cross. So now we can enjoy friendship with a Holy God. In Romans 5:10-11 we read, "For since our friendship with God was restored by the death of his Son while we were still his enemies, we will certainly be saved through the life of his Son. So now we can rejoice in our wonderful new relationship with God because our Lord Jesus Christ has made us friends of God."

Through Christ you hold a backstage VIP pass to the God of the universe! He waits with joy to help you through the storms of life.

Jeremiah understood the importance of placing His hope and confidence in God—not just occasionally, but daily. We get a peek into Jeremiah's heart through his prayers. He not only wrote the book of the Bible containing the most words but he also penned the Book of Lamentations, which follows the Book of Jeremiah. It contains his laments. A "lament" is a passionate expression of sorrow; it involves looking back on grief or devastation and shedding tears. In the midst of Lamentations is a famous text that cannot be overlooked when talking about hope in the midst of despair:

> Yet I still dare to hope
> when I remember this:
>
> The faithful love of the Lord never ends!
> His mercies never cease.
> Great is his faithfulness;

God has not abandoned us! *When it seems like all hope is lost, He is still our God.*

his mercies begin afresh each morning.
I say to myself, "The LORD is my inheritance;
therefore, I will hope in him!"

The LORD is good to those who depend on him,
to those who search for him.
So it is good to wait quietly
for salvation from the LORD.
And it is good for people to submit at an early age
to the yoke of his discipline.
(Lamentations 3:21-27)

God has not abandoned us! When it seems like all hope is lost, He is still our God. He has good plans for us, and those plans involve our living with purpose. Instead of running through life trying to get it all done, we need to slow down and live with care. We need to remember to hope, knowing that we have a Redeemer who has paid for all our sins. He has good works planned in advance for us and wants us to live in the light of His return. In other words, the fact that Jesus will come again should affect the way we live today, tomorrow, and the next day. It gives us meaning and urgency for pursuing a close relationship with Him.

Remember that God is more apt to forget about the laws of nature, such as gravity, than He is to forget about us. He sees us. He wants us to know Him intimately. He is even willing to allow difficulty in our lives to bring us back into relationship with Him when we stray. God wants us to put away our idols, cling to Him like underwear, get on the right path, and stop blaming others when we mess up. His plans are not to harm us but to give us a future and a hope (Jeremiah 29:11). Let's humble ourselves before our God and live like He is the source of our hope, *because He is*! No matter what your circumstances may be today, He invites you to dare to hope in Him. While your circumstances may not be hopeful, your God offers you steadfast love that never ceases and mercies that never end. Great is His faithfulness!

Dare to Hope Challenge

Intimacy with Jesus involves living for Him alone in a spirit of humility, trusting that His plans for you are good and believing that everything you need for living a victorious life is found in Him. What can make it difficult for you to live this out and find true intimacy with Jesus? Identify anything that may be creating distance in your relationship with Him right now—whether it's a thought, attitude, relationship, habit, or activity—and choose one thing you can do to address this obstacle. If possible, talk about it with a trusted, godly friend or mentor who can listen, pray with you, and provide friendly accountability.

EPILOGUE

Living with Intention

Set your minds on things above, not earthly things.
—Colossians 3:2 NIV

In today's unstable world, it can be difficult to hold on to hope. It's a daring thing to hope, especially when it's so easy to inadvertently set our minds on worry, despair, and bitterness as we're reading or watching the news, scrolling through social media, or even listening to conversations about all that is happening in our world. But our glimpse into Jeremiah's book and messages has shown us that as the people of God, we are called to set our minds on things above—to keep hope alive, not only for ourselves but also for the sake of the world. We are called to live for God alone and not to fall prey to the "gods" of the world that surround us. If we are daring enough to keep our ears and eyes open to God, we can be sure that God will guide us faithfully each and every day.

Living with hope—which is expecting God to move and restore wholeness where there is brokenness—is countercultural. It's countercultural to trust that God holds all things together—the good and the bad. It's countercultural to look for the places where God is moving and then jump into the flow of His Spirit. Yet what we've seen through our journey together is that hope is not simply lollipops and roses but an intentional and determined approach to every day that says, "*The*

God of the Universe has called me His own, and that means something about the way I will live my life."

My challenge for each of us is that we would dare to hope when it feels that hope is lost. Let's be the ones who shine the light and point others to the Living Hope, Jesus Christ!

Because living with intention is a daily practice, I've pulled together a few hope memory verses and a few spiritual practices that might help guide you to live with hope every day. In the same way that we train our bodies for marathons, we can train our minds and hearts to seek God. Intentional, daily practice will help us set our minds on things above. I hope you'll take the challenge and dare to hope in this unstable world!

Hope Memory Verses

"Even a tree has more hope!
    If it is cut down, it will sprout again
    and grow new branches.
Though its roots have grown old in the earth
    and its stump decays,
at the scent of water it will bud
    and sprout again like a new seedling."

(Job 14:7-9)

Lead me by your truth and teach me,
    for you are the God who saves me.
    All day long I put my hope in you.

(Psalm 25:5)

Let your unfailing love surround us, LORD,
    for our hope is in you alone.

(Psalm 33:22)

Why am I discouraged?
  Why is my heart so sad?
I will put my hope in God!
  I will praise him again—
  my Savior and my God!

(Psalm 42:11)

O Lord, you alone are my hope.
  I've trusted you, O LORD, from childhood.

(Psalm 71:5)

But I will keep on hoping for your help;
  I will praise you more and more.

(Psalm 71:14)

You are my refuge and my shield;
  your word is my source of hope.

(Psalm 119:114)

LORD, sustain me as you promised, that I may live!
  Do not let my hope be crushed.

(Psalm 119:116)

"For I know the plans I have for you," says the LORD. "They are plans for good and not for disaster, to give you a future and a hope.

(Jeremiah 29:11)

As for me, I look to the LORD for help.
  I wait confidently for God to save me,
  and my God will certainly hear me.

(Micah 7:7)

We can rejoice, too, when we run into problems and trials, for we know that they help us develop endurance. And endurance develops strength of character, and character strengthens our confident hope of salvation. And this hope will not lead to disappointment. For we know how dearly God loves us, because he has given us the Holy Spirit to fill our hearts with his love. (Romans 5:3-5)

Rejoice in our confident hope. Be patient in trouble, and keep on praying. (Romans 12:12)

I pray that God, the source of hope, will fill you completely with joy and peace because you trust in him. Then you will overflow with confident hope through the power of the Holy Spirit.
(Romans 15:13)

Let us hold tightly without wavering to the hope we affirm, for God can be trusted to keep his promise. (Hebrews 10:23)

5 Spiritual Practices for Living with Hope

1. First Thing

Before you reach for your phone in the morning or put your feet on the ground, set your heart and mind on things above. Take a few deep breaths, and then pray this breath prayer five times to set your heart on God. As you breathe in pray, "Lord of this day." As you breathe out pray, "I put all my hope in you." (Feel free to repeat the deep breaths and breath prayer throughout the day as needed!)

2. Daily Review

At the end of each day, take a few minutes to review the events of the day and ask yourself these questions: How did I sense God's presence today? Where did I see God at work today? Where did I see evidence or signs of hope? Say a prayer offering your thanks and praise for these good gifts and ask God to help you live with hope tomorrow.

3. Weekly Theme Word

As you plan for the coming week, choose a word that will be your theme or focus for the week. Let it be a word that helps to set your heart on hope—such as *hope*, *mercy*, *grace*, *love*, *forgiveness*, *intentional*, or *trust*. Write the word on several note cards and place them around your house or office where you will see them often. You also might use the word to create a screen saver for your computer or cell phone.

4. Weekly Scripture Verse

Each week select one of the Hope Memory Verses (or another verse on hope of your choosing) and write it on a note card that you can carry in your purse or wallet—or a note in your phone. Whenever you find yourself with downtime while waiting throughout the day, read over the verse and work on memorizing it. You also might begin and end the day by reciting and meditating on the verse for one minute.

5. Contingency Plan

When plans change unexpectedly or when our expectations aren't met, we can either lean in to hope or fall into despair. By choosing to live an intentional life, we are better equipped when our plans don't work out as expected. Spend a few minutes considering some scenarios that cause you to lose your focus on the faithfulness of God. Maybe you lose it in highway traffic or when your kids or coworkers don't do what you ask of them. Maybe you lose it when you see a friend's political rant on social media. What are the things that take *your* eyes off of the Source of your hope? When you know what they are, you can plan ahead to fix your eyes on Jesus.

Memorize Romans 12:12 (one of the hope memory verses), and repeat it to yourself—or say it out loud—whenever you feel yourself turning your eyes to the things of the earth: "Rejoice in our confident hope. Be patient in trouble, and keep on praying" (Romans 12:12).

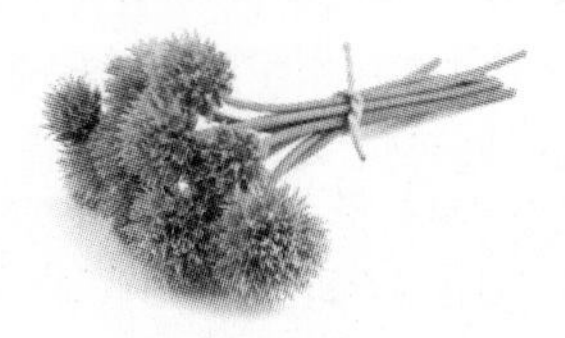

Notes

Introduction

1. Francis Schaeffer, *Death in the City* (Wheaton, IL: Crossway Books, 2002), 33.

1. Raising the White Flag

1. Jennifer Degler, "What's Wrong with Nice Girls?" Life Today website, June 5, 2011, http://lifetoday.org/connect/words-of-life/whats-wrong-with-nice-girls/.

2. Craig Groeschel, *The Christian Atheist: Believing in God but Living as if He Doesn't Exist* (Grand Rapids: Zondervan, 2010), 135.

3. Bible Study Tools, s.v. "shuwb," www.biblestudytools.com/lexicons/hebrew/kjv/shuwb.html.

4. Bible Hub, s.v. "batach," http://biblehub.com/hebrew/983.htm.

2. Recognizing Counterfeits and the Real Deal

1. Timothy Keller, *Counterfeit Gods: The Empty Promises of Money, Sex, and Power, and the Only Hope That Matters* (New York: Penguin, 2009), xvii.

2. Keller, 23–24.

3. Keller, 17.

4. See "Fact of the Week" at www.unicef.org/factoftheweek/index_53356.html and Anup Shah, "Today, Around 21,000 Children Died Around the

World," Global Issues website, September 24, 2011, www.globalissues.org /article/715/today-21000-children-died-around-the-world.

5. Lucy Elkins, "As the Number of Young People with Bowel Cancer Doubles," Daily Mail Online, April 27, 2010, www.dailymail.co.uk/health /article-1269088/Bowel-cancer-Doctors-told-Vicky-IBS-fact-tumor-size-orange.html.

3. Opening Our Ears

1. Bible Study Tools, s.v. "shama," www.biblestudytools.com/lexicons /hebrew/kjv/shama.html.

2. "The Shema," www.hebrew4christians.com/Scripture/Torah/The _Shema/the_shema.html.

3. Bible Study Tools, s.v. "yatsar," www.biblestudytools.com/lexicons /hebrew/kjv/yatsar-2.html.

4. Bible Study Tools, s.v. "Lord Sabaoth," www.biblegateway.com /resources/dictionaries/dict_meaning.php?source=1&wid=T0003169.

5. Warren W. Wiersbe, *Be Amazed: Restoring an Attitude of Wonder and Worship* (Wheaton, IL: Victor, 1996), 176.

6. Bible Study Tools, s.v. "dabaq," www.biblestudytools.com/lexicons /hebrew/kjv/dabaq.html.

7. Ralph Gower, *The New Manners and Customs of Bible Times* (Chicago: Moody, 2005), 328.

8. Frank Gaebelein, ed., The Expositors Bible Commentary, vol. 6, Isaiah, Jeremiah, Lamentations, Ezekiel (Grand Rapids: Zondervan, 1986), 524.

4. Staying Spiritually Sensitive

1. Bible Study Tools, s.v. "shama," www.biblestudytools.com/lexicons /hebrew/kjv/shama.html.

2. Bible Study Tools, s.v. "chaciyd," www.biblestudytools.com/lexicons /hebrew/kjv/chaciyd.html.

3. Marilyn Hontz, *Shame Lifter: Replacing Your Fears and Tears with Forgiveness, Truth, and Hope* (Carol Stream, IL: Tyndale, 2009), xviii.

5. Quitting the Blame Game

1. Edward Mote, "My Hope Is Built," *The United Methodist Hymnal* (Nashville: The United Methodist Publishing House, 1989), 368, refrain.

2. John Lee Hancock, dir., *The Rookie* (Burbank, CA: Walt Disney Pictures, 2002).

3. Ralph Gower, *The New Manners and Customs of Bible Times* (Chicago: Moody, 2005), 215.

4. Philip J. King, *Jeremiah: An Archaeological Companion* (Louisville: Westminster John Knox, 1993), 12.

6. Finding the Source of Our Hope

1. Bible Study Tools, s.v. "ra,'" www.biblestudytools.com/lexicons /hebrew/nas/ra.html.

2. Bible Study Tools, s.v. "mar," www.biblestudytools.com/lexicons /hebrew/nas/mar.html.

3. Edward T. Welch, *When People Are Big and God Is Small* (Phillipsburg, NJ: P&R, 1997), 123.

4. C. S. Lewis, *The Problem of Pain* (San Francisco: HarperCollins, 1940), 91.

5. Chad Brand, Charles Draper, and Archie England, eds., *Holman Illustrated Bible Dictionary* (Nashville: Holman, 2003), 1374.

6. Bible Study Tools, s.v., "Jehovah Tsidkenu," www.biblestudytools.com /dictionary/jehovah-tsidkenu/.

7. Philip Yancey, *What's So Amazing About Grace?* (Grand Rapids: Zondervan, 1997), 71.

About the Author

Melissa Spoelstra is a popular women's conference speaker (including the Aspire Women's Events), Bible teacher, and writer who is madly in love with Jesus and passionate about studying God's Word and helping women of all ages seek Christ and know Him more intimately through serious Bible study. Melissa, who has a degree in Bible theology, enjoys teaching God's Word to the body of Christ and traveling to diverse groups and churches across the nation and around the world, even to Nairobi, Kenya, for a women's prayer conference. Melissa is the author of the Bible studies *Elijah: Spiritual Stamina in Every Season*, *Numbers: Learning Contentment in a Culture of More*, *First Corinthians: Living Love When We Disagree*, *Joseph: The Journey to Forgiveness*, *Jeremiah: Daring to Hope in an Unstable World*, and the parenting books *Total Family Makeover: 8 Steps to Making Disciples at Home* and *Total Christmas Makeover: 31 Devotions to Celebrate with Purpose*. She has published articles in *ParentLife*, *Women's Spectrum*, and *Just Between Us* and writes a regular blog in which she shares her musings about what God is teaching her on any given day. She lives in Dublin, Ohio, with her pastor husband, Sean, and their four kids: Zach, Abby, Sara, and Rachel.

Follow Melissa:

Twitter	@MelSpoelstra
Instagram	@Daring2Hope
Facebook	@AuthorMelissaSpoelstra
Her blog	MelissaSpoelstra.com (check here also for event dates and booking information)

Also From Melissa Spoelstra

30 Days of Prayer for Spiritual Stamina
Paperback | 9781501874352 | $9.99
E-book | 9781501874369 | $9.99

Total Family Makeover: 8 Practical Steps to Making Disciples at Home
Paperback | 9781501820656 | $16.99
E-Book | 9781501820663 | $16.99

Total Christmas Makeover: 31 Devotions to Celebrate with Purpose
Paperback | 9781501848704 | $16.99
E-book ISBN | 9781501848711 | $16.99

Praise

"We are happy to award deserving books like *Total Family Makeover*. Our panel of judges really felt this book merited a place on our list of the best in family-friendly products that parents can feel confident in using."
—**Dawn Matheson**, Executive Director, Mom's Choice Awards

"This book [*Total Christmas Makeover*] is light fun and straight to the point with ideas I could actually do with my family. It's a must-read for anyone who starts to freak out when they even hear the word holiday!"
—**Kerri Pomarolli**, author, comedian, Hollywood actress

Did you like *Dare to Hope* or other books by Melissa Spoelstra?
Please share a review at your favorite online retailer or social media platform.

AbingdonWomen.com

Praise

"Melissa has a wonderful way of making the book of Jeremiah come alive, not only in our heads but also in our hearts."

—**Marilyn Hontz**, author of *Shame Lifter* and *Listening to God*

"'Seek God, obey God, love God' is Melissa's message to us through this deeply relevant study of Elijah. I can't wait to study this with my women's ministry!"

—**Stephanie Bringa**, Connections Director, Community Christian Church, Tamara, FL